SPECTACULAR WINERIES
of Napa Valley

A CAPTIVATING TOUR OF ESTABLISHED, ESTATE AND BOUTIQUE WINERIES

Published by

PANACHE

PANACHE PARTNERS, LLC

13747 Montfort Drive, Suite 100
Dallas, Texas 75240
972.661.9884
Fax: 972.661.2743
www.panache.com

Publishers: Brian G. Carabet and John A. Shand
Executive Publisher: Phil Reavis
Senior Publisher: Kathryn Newell
Editor: Kate Jones
Contributing Editor: Amanda Weko
Photographer: M.J. Wickham
Designer: Emily A. Kattan

Printed in Malaysia

Distributed by Independent Publishers Group
800.888.4741

PUBLISHER'S DATA

Spectacular Wineries of Napa Valley

Library of Congress Control Number: 2007930557

ISBN 13: 978-1-933415-40-6
ISBN 10: 1-933415-40-1

First Printing 2007

10 9 8 7 6 5 4 3 2 1

Previous Page: Spottswoode Estate Vineyard & Winery
See page 200 *Photograph by M.J. Wickham*

This Page: Chateau Montelena Winery
See page 68 *Photograph by M.J. Wickham*

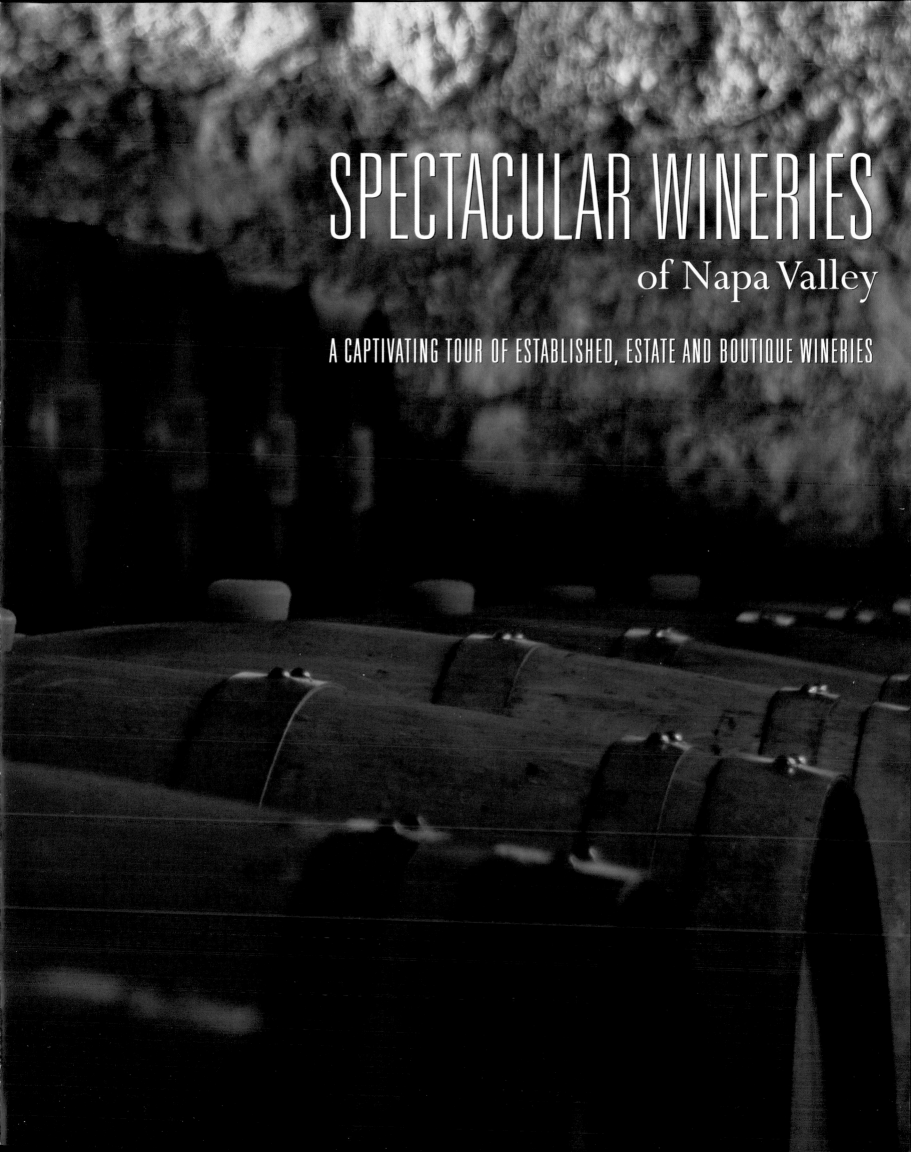

SPECTACULAR WINERIES
of Napa Valley

A CAPTIVATING TOUR OF ESTABLISHED, ESTATE AND BOUTIQUE WINERIES

Robert Mondavi Winery, *page 180*

Robert and I have enjoyed a long and wonderful love affair with the Napa Valley. For Robert, it began when his family purchased a winery here in the early 1940s. For me, it started when I became involved in Robert's winery in the 1960s. Our collaboration further ignited a shared passion for wine, food and the arts—lighting the way to a vision that has taken us on a remarkable journey marked by many exciting and beautiful memories and milestones, and many wonderful people.

The Robert Mondavi Winery became the first large-scale winery established in the valley since before Prohibition. Robert was committed to producing quality wines—on a par with France and Italy. Many wineries followed and as the Napa Valley grew, so did the region's reputation. Our iconic mission-style winery has been a benchmark for so many wineries who recognized that winery architecture can play an important role in the industry itself.

Today, Napa produces some of the finest wines in the world, as evidenced in the Judgment of Paris—first held in 1976, and simultaneously recreated in 2006 at Copia: The American Center for Wine, Food & the Arts in Napa, and Berry Bros. & Rudd of London. All were resounding triumphs for Napa Valley wines, and a feather in Robert's hat for claiming it possible from the very start.

It is also a rich reward for us both to see Napa Valley flourish from a fledgling farm county to a world-renowned cultural region—possessing both a rustic and refined charm that blends agriculture and nature with an exceptional sense of quality and appreciation of wine, food and the arts. Our enthusiasm reached beyond wineries when we, together with a group of impassioned collaborators, established Copia on the banks of the Napa River as a place for visitors and community to gather and enjoy this country's diverse and abundant wine, food and arts culture.

This remarkably beautiful book, *Spectacular Wineries of Napa Valley,* offers a taste of what makes Napa Valley unique and invites you to enjoy the wonderful stories and amazing architecture that help shape the extraordinary Napa Valley experience.

We hope it will ignite a life's passion in you to share with others.

Margrit Biever Mondavi

Margrit Biever Mondavi

Robert and Margrit Mondavi

Introduction

COPIA

The American Center for Wine, Food & the Arts
by Arthur Jacobus
President, COPIA

For many, the mere mention of Napa Valley conjures up the idyllic images of mighty Cabernets, sweeping vineyard views at dusk, the faint aroma of wood-fired grills, and the gentle titillation of one's senses, enlivened by a thoughtful meal, good wine and easy conversation. As time-honored as these images of Napa Valley wine country may be, they are a relatively recent phenomenon—aroused in the late 19th-century prosperity of post-Gold Rush California; nearly destroyed by prohibition in the 1930s; and gloriously resurrected in the mid 1960s when California's wine giants roamed the valley, quietly creating monumental wines that rivaled the Old World's finest Burgundies and Bordeaux's, changing the wine world forever.

This recent, but historic emergence of America's wines on the world wine scene, led by what is now appreciated as a remarkable roster of iconic Napa Valley vintners, generated an economic boom—still heard round the world. With annual revenues of $22 billion, the American (principally California) wine industry generates an economic impact to the United States economy of $125 billion per year. Included in this has been the creation of the iconic Napa Valley wine country—replete with acres upon acres of planted vineyards, over 200 wineries, and scores of destination restaurants, hotel resorts and a growing flourish of related commerce.

At the gateway to this fabled wine country stands COPIA: The American Center for Wine, Food & the Arts—a stunning testimonial to the vision of the legendary Robert Mondavi, who many consider the tallest among the giants in American wine history.

Top Left: Copia's river concert terrace glimmers at night.
Photograph by Richard Barnes

Middle Left: Robert and Margrit Mondavi enjoy the company of Julia Child in Julia's kitchen/dining room at Copia's grand opening.
Photograph by M.J. Wickham

Bottom Left: From Copia's flourishing gardens, these tomatoes beg to be savored.
Photograph by Faith Echtermeyer

Facing Page: The rolling hills of Napa Valley fold one into another.
Photograph by M.J. Wickham

Robert Mondavi's vision, which he shared with his remarkable wife, Margrit Biever Mondavi, and the celebrated Julia Child, was to establish a destination in the heart of Napa Valley where people from all walks of life could gather to celebrate and explore the fascinating and delicious cultural intersection of wine, food and the arts through interactive programs and experiences that would engage the senses, stir the imagination, and inspire reflection, conversation and community. With this vision, and contagious generosity, Robert and Margrit Mondavi launched a campaign in the late 1990s that enlisted philanthropic support throughout the wine community, resulting in the opening of COPIA to the public in November 2001.

Situated along the banks of the Napa River, COPIA, a non-profit discovery center, is a spectacular American architectural landmark—featuring enticing vistas of its organic edible gardens and the surrounding Napa downtown community. Within its position as the nation's leading resource for consumer wine education, COPIA's wine, culinary, garden and arts experts offer the wine country visitor an innovative menu of

compelling sensory experiences, which include: wine appreciation and education programs, cooking demonstrations, garden interactions, wine/food and art festivals, live concert performances, unique exhibitions and fine dining at the acclaimed Julia's Kitchen. Finally, as a catalyst behind the transformation of Napa from a retiring farm town into a thriving center of reinvigorated commerce, COPIA anchors the emerging Oxbow District, comprised of artisan retail enterprises, cuisine and local hospitality in a fashion that beckons and equips wine country visitors to explore and discover the full gamut of experiences available throughout America's original, and most heralded wine country.

Above: The Napa River sets an elegant tone.
Photograph by Richard Barnes

Facing Page Top Left: All of the lunch wines are delectable in their own right.
Photograph by Faith Echtermeyer

Facing Page Middle Left: "Taste of COPIA" instructors freely share their expertise.
Photograph by Faith Echtermeyer

Facing Page Bottom Left: A view of the COPIA tower from the Edible Gardens.
Photograph by Faith Echtermeyer

Facing Page Right: A culinary instructor gives a demonstration at the Edible Gardens Festival.
Photograph by Faith Echtermeyer

Paramount among these experiences, and a primary draw among the four million annual visitors to Napa Valley, are the many spectacular wineries that dot the landscape across Napa's 14 wine-producing regions. While many of these wineries are accessible from the main highway and byways through the valley, some may be found nestled in the hillsides and valleys, or hidden away amidst rows of planted Cabernet and Chardonnay.

Much like the wines of Napa Valley, the valley's winery architecture is rich and varied—sometimes a reflection of intended wine brand imagery; and other times, a manifestation of the dreams, vision or passions of their respective founders and owners. As such, with every twist and turn through the county's meandering thoroughfares, the visitor may be greeted by a surprising array of invitations to their senses that may compel them to gaze, wonder, admire, or as many wineries would have it, stop by for wine tasting, tours, casual conversation and shopping!

While many of these wineries are open to the public, some are accessible by invitation only. Moreover, with over 200 wineries in Napa Valley, many visitors aspire to take in more wineries than time

allows (four to five wineries in a single day is ambitious for most). For these wine enthusiasts, and others who may simply enjoy and appreciate the aesthetics of, and story behind splendidly inspired architecture, this arresting book, *Spectacular Wineries of Napa Valley,* is so intended.

In this regard, we at COPIA are pleased to partner with Panache Partners, LLC to present this sumptuous salute to the story and architecture of some of Napa Valley's most spectacular wineries.

Bon Appétit!

Above: History-making of judges and vintners attend the 30th Anniversary celebration of the Judgment of Paris—at COPIA.
Photograph by Faith Echtermeyer

Facing Page Left: COPIA's stunning water allée entrance welcomes all to experience the finest in wine, food and the arts.
Photograph by Faith Echtermeyer

Facing Page Top Right: A variety of extraordinary wines await tasting at the Judgment of Paris
Photograph by Faith Echtermeyer

Facing Page Bottom Right: These corks, from the Judgment of Paris, will long be cherished.
Photograph by Faith Echtermeyer

From the Publisher

As I drive into the Napa Valley a feeling of calm comes over me and I realize that this is a very special place. You can't help falling in love with the Napa Valley. It has a personality all its own. The colors are like a painter's palette—always changing with the season—from the bright yellows of mustard plants in the spring, the greens of summer grape leaves, to the fall harvest colors of burgundy and rust, followed by the quiet shades of brown and black in winter. The morning fog, afternoon sun, moderate temperatures and the talents of vintners and growers combine to produce world-class wines. All share a common goal of respecting the land and nurturing the fruit that each distinct terroir produces.

This small slice of heaven on earth is only 30 miles long and five miles wide, enticing the public to view the life of wine making and incredible cuisine all while enjoying the relaxed and laid back lifestyle of small-town living. People are happy here and they show it. A passerby says good morning, cars pause while drivers wave you to cross the street, everything moves at a slow and kind pace. You find that you are smiling for no reason. It is truly a magical setting.

You enter the Napa Valley by one of two roads: Route 29 or the Silverado Trail. Both offer you great access to the valley floor wineries, restaurants and charming small towns. Some of the best-kept secrets are hidden in the valley hills. Venture off the beaten path to discover wineries tucked away in canyons or perched on the mountaintops with 360-degree views that take your breath away, all with a slightly diverse climate that makes all the difference when it comes to creating a spectacular wine. This varied collection of wineries celebrates the art of wine making as well as the art, architecture, culture, heritage and way of life that for centuries has graced this area.

Spectacular Wineries of Napa Valley takes you on a journey of 46 world-class wineries. Each has a unique story told by the vintners and owners themselves, with photography that invites you into their world. Our goal is to educate you about the types of wineries and their diversity in size, style and blends. We'll tell you the story behind the wineries that are as delectable as the wines they produce. We offer a rare look into cult wines such as J.P. Harbison Wines, Stony Hill or new releases like Ackerman Family Vineyards and Jaffe Estate Wines; we have wineries that are by appointment only—Barnett Vineyards, David Arthur and Spottswoode—as well as public wineries including Beringer, Chateau Montelena, Robert Mondavi and Charles Krug.

I have been to every one of these wineries, each different, yet alike. Every one produces outstanding, if not award-winning wine while offering gracious hospitality and sharing an immense passion for wine. Sit back and enjoy a glass of your favorite wine and journey into this firsthand world in *Spectacular Wineries of Napa Valley*.

Cheers,

Kathryn Newell

Kathryn Newell
Senior Publisher

Photograph by Carol Bates

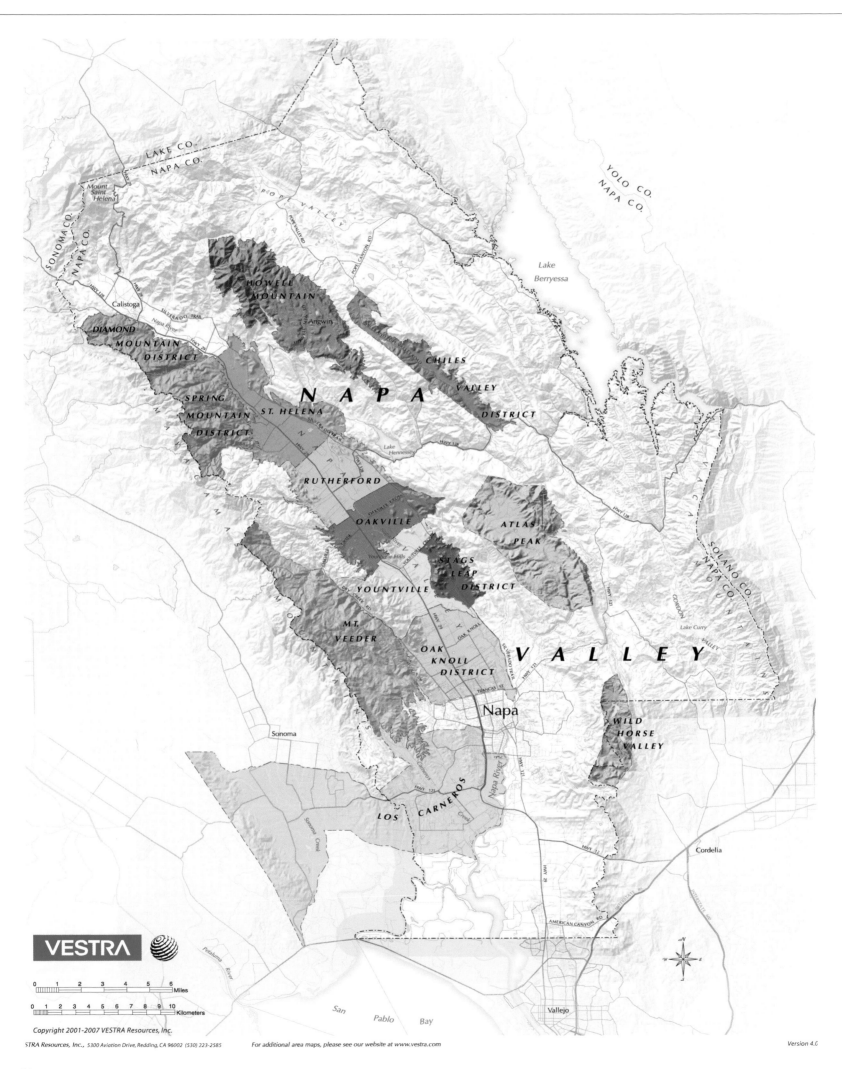

LAKE CO.
NAPA CO.

YOLO CO.
NAPA CO.

Mount Saint Helena

Lake Berryessa

SONOMA CO.
NAPA CO.

HOWELL MOUNTAIN

Calistoga

DIAMOND MOUNTAIN DISTRICT

Angwin

CHILES VALLEY DISTRICT

SPRING MOUNTAIN DISTRICT

ST. HELENA

N A P A

Lake Hennessey

RUTHERFORD

OAKVILLE

ATLAS PEAK

STAGS LEAP DISTRICT

YOUNTVILLE

MT. VEEDER

OAK KNOLL DISTRICT

V A L L E Y

Napa

Sonoma

WILD HORSE VALLEY

Lake Curry

LOS CARNEROS

Cordelia

San Pablo Bay

Vallejo

Table of Contents

Wine to me is passion. It's family and friends. It's warmth of heart and generosity of spirit. Wine is art. It's culture. It's the essence of civilization and of the art of living.

—from *Harvests of Joy* by Robert Mondavi

Napa Valley

Ackerman Family Vineyards

Napa

A pristine 1941 Chevy pulls up in front of the Napa Valley restaurant carrying precious cargo. Bob Ackerman disembarks to unload the Ackerman Family Vineyards Cabernet that he personally delivers to local accounts.

Bob enjoys driving his truck around Napa Valley and knows the 80-year-old man who completely rebuilt it—four years in the making—would get a kick out of it, too. His wife, Lauren, found this dream-truck on the Internet, surprising her husband on his birthday.

Finding a truck on the Internet and shipping it cross-country might be daunting to some, but not to Lauren, who worked in the high-tech industry before starting work in the non-profit sector in Napa Valley. She's currently chairman of the Napa Valley Community Foundation, a philanthropic "bank" for philanthropic donors who come together to determine what the strongest needs in a community are, funding grants accordingly. All net profits from the sales of Ackerman Family Vineyards Cabernet go to the Community Foundation. When not making and delivering wine, Bob, a wine connoisseur since his early 20s, works as a venture capitalist and managing director at the firm he founded.

Napa Valley was always a special place for Bob and Lauren. Having exchanged wedding vows in the wine country in 1989, they vowed that someday they would move there. That day came in July of 1994, when Bob was looking to buy a horse for Lauren. At the time, he went to a Napa Valley property to see a horse, and the owners mentioned they were also selling their property. The Ackermans bought the house and vineyard, and the sellers gave them the two horses. Today, Lauren enjoys an occasional ride through the vineyard while also breeding and showing quarter horses and Western pleasure paints.

Top Left: Enjoying the Ackerman Family's Cabernet Sauvignon on a warm afternoon.

Bottom Left: Entrance to Ackerman Family Vineyards.

Facing Page: Looking west over the vineyard after a hail storm.

Their two sons, Robert and Alex, grew up playing in the vineyard—for them, it became a way of life.

Since becoming vintners, they have tirelessly worked the vineyard, learning its nuances through trellising, pruning, installing irrigation and replanting. In 1998, they began replanting all 11 acres to Cabernet Sauvignon on drought-resistant rootstock and changed the trellis system to create more harmony with the terroir. Replanting the vineyard in thirds meant they always had grapes to make a few barrels of wine for themselves, as well as enough to share with friends and restaurants. In 2003, the Ackermans created their first commercial vintage at the urging of local friends already in the wine business who felt it was "time."

They farm the vineyard organically, using cover crops and composting. They've also made friends with predators of the air, utilizing hawk boxes to keep rodents out of the vineyard. Alex, their child-entrepreneur, keeps in the family spirit with his organic egg-farming business called "Alex's Eggzactly Organic."

The Ackermans don't run a typical winery. There isn't a tasting room to visit or a facility tour to take. Marketing involves pouring at

Top Left: Bob, Alex and Lauren inspect the vines.

Middle Left: Lauren takes Gracie, her Western pleasure show horse out for a walk in the vineyard.

Bottom Left: Bob's 1941 Chevy delivery truck.

Facing Page: Looking through the olive trees to the vineyard beyond.

tasting events and non-profit fundraisers. Their wine is sold direct through their Web site. Those fortunate enough to taste the Ackerman Family Vineyards Cabernet are treated to nuances of chocolate interspersed with raspberry, giving way to a smooth texture. It is a wine crafted to age gracefully or enjoy any time.

Small is the way this family wants to keep it. "We make wines for our own taste. It holds up well over the years," shares Lauren. "One of our greatest pleasures is to be together at a meal of organic food drinking our wine, enjoying the moment."

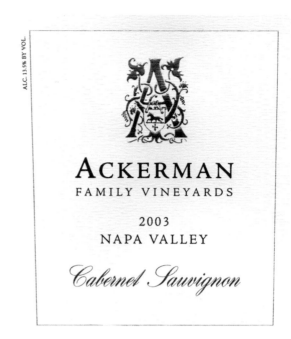

ALC. 13.5% BY VOL.

ACKERMAN
FAMILY VINEYARDS

2003
NAPA VALLEY

Cabernet Sauvignon

Barlow Vineyards

Calistoga

Barlow Vineyards is reminiscent of an earlier era in Napa Valley. When guests make an appointment to visit, Warren Smith, co-founder of Barlow Vineyards, opens his home for their hospitality. Tasters may sample the small-production estate wines either in Warren's elegant, open-beamed living room or, when it is sunny, on the deck that offers a spectacular view of neat rows of vineyards and the mountains beyond. It is a warm, personal experience, vastly different from a traditional tasting room.

The Smiths always had a feeling of belonging in Napa Valley, as the family began coming up to the area in 1954 from Southern California. They made annual trips and frequently came many times a year. "I watched Napa Valley wine evolve," says Warren. "I remember bringing my young son Barr along when my wife, Jeanne, and I went wine tasting. He would sit on the wine cartons at Louis Martini Winery. The staff would get the glasses out of the broom closet." These fond memories were the seeds of inspiration for Barlow Vineyards.

When Warren retired from the pharmaceutical industry, he did not like retirement and asked his son, Barr, and daughter-in-law, Ann, to be partners in a vineyard. In 1994, the two generations bought their 50-acre Napa Valley property, just below Calistoga on the Silverado Trail. It was a dream fulfilled. Warren and Jeanne had looked at the property for years as a place they would like to live, long before it became available to be purchased.

Intending to focus solely on viticulture, their original plan was to grow grapes for other wineries. Some of the 36 acres of vineyards and trellis systems were replaced. On this

Top Left: Warren and Barr Smith.

Bottom Left: Big bold reds are what you will find at Barlow.

Facing Page: Spectacular views of Barlow Vineyards.

downward-sloping, wind-protected area, Cabernet Sauvignon and Merlot vines trained to the Open Lyre system enjoy maximum air and sun exposure. The warmer microclimate at Barlow in the northern end of the valley particularly suits red varietals—no white grapes are grown. The Perkins Loam soil—lava rock and fine loam—drains well. The elements combine to produce the powerful, concentrated flavors that fully express the goût de terroir (taste of the land) so prized in Barlow grapes and revealed in the wines.

Barlow Vineyards' focus changed in 1997. "Our winery came to be as the result of our making a small amount of Cabernet Sauvignon, originally meant for our family to enjoy," Warren relates. "Our winemaker informed us that the mere half-ton of 100-percent single-vineyard fruit had produced an outstanding wine; it was big

bodied, with marvelous flavors and finish and a great mouth feel." He suggested that the Smiths release the wine, and even though it was a modest 25 cases, "It was an instant success!"

The Estate Cabernet Sauvignon, the largest of their very limited production, is a fine representation of their hands-on wine growing. Their Cabernet is opaque; the nose rich in aromas of black sour cherry with hints of sweet vanilla that is a direct reflection of French oak barrels. Full-bodied, the palate is laden with lush black currant and sweet jam, the finish long, with luxurious tannins. Barlow Vineyards

Above Left: Make yourself at home while visiting Barlow Vineyards.

Above Right: Fabulous views are part of the experience.

Facing Page: Barlow Vineyards' 50 acres are on the Silverado Trail just south of Calistoga.

keeps wine production small to achieve optimum quality, using only 15 percent of the vineyard's total yield for their premier estate wines. Quintessential winegrowers, the family continues to sell their sought-after grapes to well-known Napa Valley wineries.

BARLOW

Barnett Vineyards

St. Helena

Fiona and Hal Barnett first discovered Spring Mountain in 1983 while they were living in San Francisco. At the time, they came across 40 acres of undeveloped forested land at 2,000 feet elevation, overlooking the Napa Valley below. One year later, after clearing the land and terracing the vineyards, the Barnetts planted 6,000 vines of Cabernet Sauvignon. In 1989, after careful years of farming and planning, the first vintage of Barnett Vineyards produced 300 cases of Spring Mountain Estate Cabernet Sauvignon.

At this point, the Barnetts' vision was to produce small amounts of wine to be enjoyed by them and their friends. This vision soon changed as the wines being made from this intimate piece of land gained importance as one of Napa Valley's known Cabernet Sauvignons. Since 1990, Hal and Fiona have lived full time at the estate raising their three daughters. While Hal was engaged in his construction development company, Fiona, a CPA, began focusing on building the wine business. Over the years, the production has grown to 6,000 cases annually and the vineyard has expanded to over 12,000 vines. Though they make several vineyard-designated varietals, their Rattlesnake Hill and Spring Mountain District Cabernet Sauvignons are the Barnett Vineyards' flagship wines, produced from the powerful and intense fruit for which the appellation is famous.

Vineyards always precede wines, and planting the vines on the top of a mountain was a challenge. They carefully chose vineyard sites on the 40-acre estate. Sloped at a 30-degree angle or more, building terraces for the vineyards was the most practical plan to prepare the estate for planting.

Top Left: Hal and Fiona Barnett enjoy another beautiful day in paradise.
Photograph courtesy of Barnett Vineyards

Middle Left: Picturesque view of the backyard residence and rose garden.
Photograph courtesy of Barnett Vineyards

Bottom Left: These alluring bottles hold Napa Valley's finest.

Facing Page: This gracious, shaded courtyard is an idyllic place for tastings, with its commanding fountain and lush foliage.

Top: Rattlesnake Hill and the winery are seen from a westerly view.

Bottom: The French oak barrels of this striking barrel room house Spring Mountain Cabernets and Merlots for approximately two years.

Top: This poolside terrace overlooks the magnificent Napa Valley.

Bottom: Vineyards surround the winery and tasting room.

The topography is steep and the plantings closely spaced, so traditional farming methods such as tractors and disking are not possible. These hard-to-access vines are cultivated completely by hand, tending them from bud-break in early spring until they are hand-harvested in the fall. The well-ordered pattern of vine rows nestles within the black oak, madrone, redwood and fir trees that share the top of this mountain. An observation deck atop Rattlesnake Hill provides a view of the terraced estate vineyards and magnificent views of the Napa Valley floor below.

Soil, rainfall and temperature contribute to the celebrated flavor of Spring Mountain Cabernet Sauvignon. The summit of Spring Mountain receives twice as much rain as the valley floor, averaging 60 inches during the rainy season. The soil on the property is known as Aiken Soil, the majority of which has eroded into the valley floor over the millennium. The vines work harder in this harsh environment to produce fruit, resulting in lower yields and smaller more intensely flavored berries.

While grapes planted on the valley floor thrive under the cooling marine-influenced fog that daily rolls up the valley as a foil for the hot days, Barnett Vineyards is a good 10 degrees cooler due to the altitude. The vineyards are above the fog line and flourish in the extra hours of sunlight. At night an inversion layer develops. "In the evenings it is warmer on the mountain than in the valley," Hal says.

With passion and patience, the Barnetts created this vineyard and winery with the intent of producing small amounts of hand-crafted Cabernet Sauvignon wines from this beautiful estate on Spring Mountain. Spring

Left: A spectacular view of the Valley is afforded while picnicking on the lower terrace.

Facing Page: Looking eastward, the original 25-year-old Cabernet vineyards are terraced along the hillside.

Mountain has proven to deserve its own AVA and become known as a unique microclimate, producing exceptional Cabernet Sauvignons and Merlots.

The Barnetts are dedicated to the principles of remaining a small, 100-percent family-owned winery. The dedication of the entire Barnett Vineyards team combined with excellent grapes, careful vineyard farming and hands-on winemaking have contributed to the fulfillment of those quality objectives.

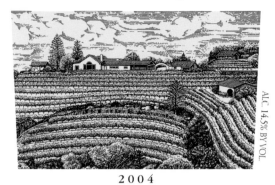

BARNETT VINEYARDS

ALC. 14.5% BY VOL.

2004

Spring Mountain District
NAPA VALLEY
CABERNET SAUVIGNON

Benessere Vineyards, Ltd.

St. Helena

Benessere is Italian for "well-being," which translates to living the good life. Having traveled to many parts of the world, winery proprietors John and Ellen Benish found a piece of this life in Napa Valley. Napa Valley's deep community roots and family values resonated with their Midwestern upbringing, so in 1994 they restored a piece of property in St. Helena that had once been a dairy farm and stables, and in its first life was home to the Wappo Native American Indians. In fact, you can still find arrowheads on the property.

Since the Benishes are part-time residents, they needed a winemaker who could manage all aspects of the wine business. In 1995, they hired well-known Napa Valley winemaker and general manager Chris Dearden. Dearden, trained in Enology at UC Davis and with an MBA from UC Berkeley, is a hands-on winemaker known for his careful attention to detail. Together, they are committed to creating Italian-inspired wines of excellence.

Although St. Helena is known for its Cabernet, Benessere initially took a gamble on planting Sangiovese, a wine rising in popularity. The soil and climate appeared to be well-suited for growing this difficult varietal. Partnering with world-renowned Italian wine consultant Dr. Alberto Antonini, the expertise of Chris Dearden has helped them achieve this goal. Antonini consults globally and continues to add an educated palate for blending their Italian inspired wines.

Top Left: Winery proprietors John and Ellen Benish.
Photograph by Hanson Fong

Bottom Left: General manager and winemaker Chris Dearden.

Facing Page: A view of the estate winery and home across Benessere's 42 acres of vineyards.

Over the years, they evolved to other Italian varietals, including Pinot Grigio, Aglianico, Sagrantino, Muscat di Canelli, plus Zinfandel and Syrah. Today, Benessere is a popular small-production boutique winery known as much for its Italian varietals as for its warm and welcoming reception.

Benessere's signature wine is its limited quantity Phenomenon blend, representing the pinnacle of its estate winemaking. This wine is a unique blend of Cabernet Sauvignon, Sangiovese, Merlot and Syrah made solely from the hand-tended estate vineyards that surround the winery. Both New and Old World ties are evident in this highly pleasing "Super Napan" wine modeled after Italy's famed Super Tuscans.

With its daily wine tastings and Buoni Amici (good friends) Wine Club, the winery aims to attract a wide audience to its wines and the Benessere way of life. Visitors enter the winery via a quiet tree-lined country road that leads to a winery surrounded by picturesque gardens, a small picnic area, and meticulously-maintained vineyards.

Top Left: Guests to the winery get a glimpse into the barrel room via Benessere's historic two story entrance doors.
Photograph by Dianne Woods

Bottom Left: The winery mascot, a Newfoundland, greets guests on the country garden patio in front of the Tasting Room.

Facing Page: Surrounded by acres of beautiful vineyards and the Mayacamas mountains, visitors discover that Benessere is truly a working boutique winery out in the country.
Photograph by Dianne Woods

The winery mascot, an imposing yet gentle Newfoundland, greets visitors and family alike. In Benessere's casual and cozy Tuscan-style tasting room, visitors are treated to a family-style atmosphere while sampling their fine quality wines and enjoying panoramic views of the surrounding hillsides and vineyards.

Here's to the good life!

Beringer Vineyards

St. Helena

Beringer—a name that evokes the past and expresses the future. The oldest continuously operating winery in the Napa Valley, the Beringer Estate sits idyllically behind a stunning tunnel of elm trees planted in 1885 by the winery founders, brothers Jacob and Frederick Beringer. A 215-acre property purchased for $14,500 in 1875 continues to be the heart of the Beringer Vineyards' Napa Valley Estate. The historic Hudson House was part of the purchase, while the famed gravity-flow winery and stone cellar were constructed throughout the next few years. Chinese laborers hand-chiseled over 1,000 linear feet of tunnels which, more than 100 years later, continue to offer efficient storing and aging facilities, maintaining an average temperature of 58° F.

The Beringer brothers came to Napa Valley from Germany. Jacob was especially exuberant to discover that the rocky, well-drained soils of Napa Valley were similar to those of his native Rhine Valley. Napa Valley's volcanic soil provided an ideal region for growing the European grape varietals he knew, and the hills could be dug out to provide the storage and aging tunnels where Beringer fine wines are aged to this day. At the entrance to the caves is the restored Old Stone Winery—a popular attraction for visitors.

In 1883, Frederick began construction of a 17-room mansion, reminiscent of the family home located on the Rhine River. He had his brother's house literally moved, using horses and logs, to make room for his "Rhine House." Restored in 1971, the Rhine House was placed on the National Register of Historic Places. It stands today as the focal point

Top Left: Beringer Vineyards is famous for its Private Reserve Chardonnay, an exceptional blend of the year's best Napa Valley vineyard lots.

Bottom Left: The gentleman's parlor room provides a historic setting to enjoy tastings in the Rhine House.

Facing Page: The Rhine House, built in 1884 as Frederick Beringer's residence, is a classic example of Victorian architecture and boasts 40 panels of stained glass.

of the Beringer Estate where guests can delight in reserve and library tastings, enjoy a glass of wine while relaxing in Frederick's library or on his porch overlooking expansive lawns and lush gardens. Jacob's house was the farmhouse, referred to as the Hudson House. It has been meticulously restored and serves as the Beringer Vineyards' Culinary Arts Center.

After surviving Prohibition (1920-1933) by selling sacramental wines, Beringer again pioneered tradition. The winery became the first to offer public tours and sales, thus launching the tourist wine business in Napa Valley. Today, visitors to the winery can participate in a variety of tours and tastings, including: Introducing Beringer Vineyards Tour, Historic District Tour, Vintage Legacy Tour, Taste of Beringer Tour, Wine & Cheese Tasting, Wine & Food Tasting and Tasting in the Cellar. All tours include specially focused wine tastings.

Beringer's Winemaster, Ed Sbragia, has been making wine at Beringer for more than 30 years. The modern pioneer of Beringer, he is leading the winery into its third century of making fine wines from Napa's outstanding

Top Left: The herb garden outside the Hudson House is just below the Old Stone Winery.

Bottom Left: The ground floor of the Rhine House serves as a tasting area and shopping destination for Beringer's many visitors throughout the year.

Facing Page: A reserve tasting room on the second floor of the Rhine House offers guests a place to enjoy Beringer's library and reserve wines for which the winery is widely respected.

appellations and vineyards. Beringer's own vineyards are the primary sources of Beringer wines. Sbragia has been, along with vineyard consultant Bob Steinhauer, the keystone of Beringer's Private Reserve Program. The Private Reserve designation is applied only to wines made with the most exacting winemaking techniques, from grapes found in the best vineyards. Ed is often heard saying, "Bob always says he gives me diamonds, and it's up to me to polish them."

BERINGER VINEYARDS

Black Coyote Chateau

Napa

The name Black Coyote represents the whimsical, yet clever, side of a dynamic winery foursome. The coyote is opportunistic by nature, generally living in packs, but hunting alone. A black coyote is a rarity. Black Coyote is a consortium of four friends who enjoy the communal pursuit of crafting fine wine, a passionate mission for each individual. Each has his own job and life pursuits, yet they work as a close-knit team in their endeavor to make approachable Napa Valley Cabernet Sauvignon and Chardonnay.

Like so many before them, the Black Coyote consortium perfectly fits into one segment of California's viticultural history. These are not people who were born or married into the business. Rather, they fall into the group of individuals with outstanding life achievements in their respective careers, who become entranced with California's wine heritage and find themselves embarking upon another chapter in their lives—making wine. They come like moths to a flame with an abundance of passion and a clear understanding that anything they do in life is always done at the highest level. Their lives are committed to constant achievement and nothing but the best will do.

Black Coyote Chateau is such an achievement for these four worldly individuals. Their chosen name, Black Coyote, is a tribute to the visiting coyote at the Bates Creek Vineyard Estate, located in Napa Valley's historic region of Coombsville. Like the rare

Top Left: In the foreground are Black Coyote Chateau's well-manicured gardens. In the background are sprawling vineyards.
Photograph by Jo Diaz

Bottom Left: Cabernet Sauvignon is planted against the Silverado Mountains on the Black Coyote Chateau property. Early morning sunlight bathes the vineyards, while slow-moving fog dissipates into the atmosphere.
Photograph by Jo Diaz

Facing Page: An inviting entrance to Black Coyote Chateau welcomes visitors to this small-production, Napa Valley wine company.

black coyote, the personalities behind Black Coyote Chateau are ingenious, intellectual and ambitious. They are: Dr. Ernest A. Bates, Dr. Olin Robison, John F. Ruffle and Stanley S. Trotman Jr. The original "black coyote" is Dr. Ernest Bates who, in 1997, moved to Napa Valley. Having always taken pleasure in fine wine, he soon caught the wine bug and started Bates Creek winery, which would ultimately evolve into the Black Coyote partnership with his three close friends.

Bates, one of the first African American neurosurgeons in the United States, is one of only a few African American vintners, and a founder of the African American Vintners Association. His friends and business partners bring an equally astounding level of business acumen to the wine consortium: Olin Robison, former president of Middlebury College and president emeritus of the Salzburg Seminar, a nonprofit organization founded after World War II to build international cooperation among young people; John F. Ruffle, a retired director and vice chairman of the board with J.P. Morgan and Co. of New York; and retired investment banker Stanley Trotman Jr., formerly a managing director with the health care group of Paine Webber, Inc.

Top Left: Flagship wine: Black Coyote Chateau Napa Valley Cabernet. As the brand developed, a Black Coyote Chardonnay was added to complement fine wine dining experiences.
Photograph by Melanie Hoffman

Bottom Left: Black Coyote Consortium, left to right: Dr. Olin Robison, John F. Ruffle, Dr. Ernest A. Bates, Stanley S. Trotman Jr.
Photograph by Jo Diaz

Facing Page: Bates Creek is located on the Black Coyote property. It's a favorite watering hole for domestic water fowl, and is frequented by many migratory birds.

Collaboratively, these "black coyotes" are enjoying the quality of life that is synonymous with Napa Valley. As they have done throughout their lives, they are bringing their passion for excellence and gracious living to the making of superlative wines, under the Black Coyote Chateau label.

Bouchaine Vineyards

Napa

Bouchaine is the oldest continuously operating winery in the Carneros District— a winery that began making wine long before the region earned its reputation for producing the great Pinot Noirs and Chardonnays of Carneros today.

Twenty-five years ago, Gerret and Tatiana Copeland discovered an old winery in what was then a little known district in Napa Valley—Los Carneros. They purchased a run-down property in an unspoiled, rural winegrowing region.

Their purchase of Bouchaine Vineyards immediately became a welcome challenge, mingling their love of business, environment, agriculture and wine. Their long-held vision for the Carneros region has been confirmed by its startling growth over the past 25 years. Situated in the southern end of the Napa Valley, Bouchaine Vineyards is located at the top of San Pablo and San Francisco Bays. The marine influence from the Bay region plays a distinctive role in the character of the wines produced in Carneros. Cool nights, foggy mornings and breezy, sunny afternoons create the perfect conditions for growing Pinot Noir and Chardonnay with depth, grace and roundness.

Today, Bouchaine Vineyards is an authentic Carneros landmark, with its three distinctive cupolas. All the exterior walls of the winery and the Visitors' Center were covered with the wood remilled from old redwood tanks, while the broad green roof gives an elegant but rustic look.

With imagination and passion, Gerret and Tatiana have fashioned wines and a wine country experience for visitors that is a distillation of their remarkable lives. At home

Top Left: Bouchaine Vineyards' three distinctive cupolas are a recognizable Carneros landmark.

Bottom Left: Tatiana and Gerret Copeland celebrate 25 years as proprietors of Bouchaine Vineyards.

Facing Page: The classic rolling hills of Carneros produce award-winning Pinot Noirs and Chardonnays with depth, grace and roundness.

in Wilmington, Delaware and in Napa Valley, the Copelands have always been very active in the world of art, music and the environment.

Gerret Copeland is Chairman of the Board at Bouchaine, where his passion for wine, his charming personal style, and his insistent focus on quality are the driving forces behind the winery's day-to-day operations. Wine has always been prominent in his life. "I have always adored the softness, fleshiness and roundness of great Pinot Noir. It is a wine of unique charms. In my family, wine was not part of our lifestyle—it was in our blood!" he says, alluding to his du Pont family's French heritage.

Above: Bouchaine's unique twin "Garretto Hills" rise from the winery's 100 acres of gently rolling estate vineyards.

Left: Guests are welcome to linger with a glass of wine on the winery's deck overlooking the breathtaking views of the expansive vineyards.
Photograph by Wendy Y Yen

In addition to her love of fine wines, as President of the winery, Tatiana Copeland brings a diverse international background to Bouchaine. Her family legacy is remarkable. Composer Sergei Rachmaninoff was her great uncle and her Russian roots go back more than 1,000 years. Born in Europe, educated in South America, fluent in five languages, her varied and colorful background influences the careful attention that is paid to providing a warm, personal and unforgettable visitor experience.

Above: The winery's walls are covered with wood from recycled and remilled old redwood wine tanks, for a rustic country look.
Photograph by Dona Kopol Bonick

Right: Visitors are greeted by ornate wrought iron gates at each entrance of Bouchaine Vineyards.

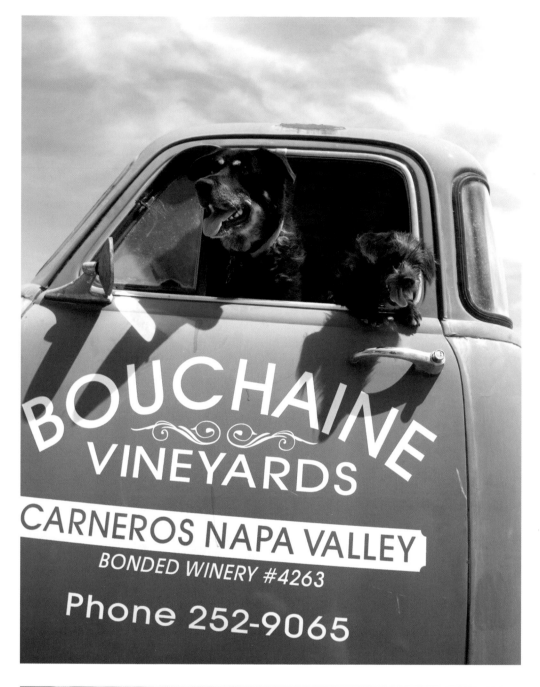

At the winery, surrounded by hundreds of acres of vineyards, guests are welcome to sit on the deck, sip a glass of wine and enjoy the serenity. "You go out on Bouchaine's terrace and feel the vineyard around you," Tatiana says. "It seduces and envelops you. Nearly everyone who comes here feels that connection. It is a connection to the soil, to the Earth. It's a very special place."

The Copelands have a long history in land preservation. Under their guardianship, the winery was one of the first to participate in the Napa Green Farm Certification program. As a "Green" winery, Bouchaine works closely with Napa County resource conservation agencies to develop a long-term plan that preserves the natural resources of the land and protects the surrounding waterways.

As great dog lovers, the Copelands endorse a dog-friendly winery. Throughout the winery, you may find a doggy bed, a dish of water and snacks! Winery mascots, Earl and D'Artagnan, love to take rides through the vineyards in the winery truck.

A distinctive component of the vineyard is the unique twin hills jutting up from the gently rolling hills of the Carneros region. Portrayed on the wine label, the "Garretto Hills" are named for the original winery founder, Johnny Garretto.

Previous Page: Bouchaine Vineyards, the oldest continuously operating winery in the Los Carneros appellation, is surrounded by hundreds of acres of vineyards offering an unforgettable wine country experience.

Top Left: Earl and D'Artagnan, the vineyard's informative staff, are on hand to greet and guide visitors through the vineyards and cellar of Bouchaine Vineyards!

Bottom Left: The changeable skies of Carneros cast color tints on the ancient redwood siding of Bouchaine Vineyards' cellar building.

Facing Page: Pinot Noir and Chardonnay—Bouchaine Vineyards' premium wines are the pride of Gerret and Tatiana Copeland, Napa Valley vintners for over 25 years.

The Copelands' vision for Bouchaine is unchanged and steadfast in their quest to produce world-class Pinot Noir and Chardonnay from Carneros. Thanks to Tatiana's business focus and Gerret's passion for wine, the winery has continued to make progress towards their ultimate goal—making great Burgundian varietal wines.

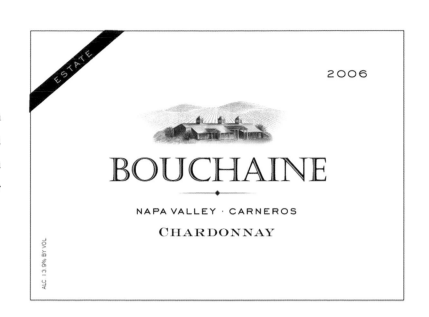

Palisades Vineyard is a strikingly beautiful place. Its 18 acres are set in a private valley northeast of Calistoga in the northern end of the Napa Valley. Stunningly peaceful views of mountains, vineyards and Horn's Creek belie the dramatic changes in weather and often extreme conditions that affect the area. Yet the property has been a productive vineyard for more than a century, dry-farmed for 90 years by Italian immigrant Domenico Barberis and his family. It has survived droughts and floods, and even Prohibition—during which time Barberis made sacramental wine for churches—producing grapes that yield rich and luxurious wine. When Anne Carver and Denis Sutro relocated from San Francisco in 1992, they sought a place to raise their four children. What they found was their own place in Napa Valley's wine history—and its future.

Carrying on the tradition of making wine from the property's 40-year-old Petite Sirah vines was a challenge Carver and Sutro aimed to meet. First, they matched the Barberis family's Old World farming style by hiring second-generation vineyard manager Josh Clark. Next, they enlisted Gary Brookman, a talented and passionate winemaker who recognized the vineyard's quality and embraced the prospect of making one of the Napa Valley's best Petite Sirahs. Together, the team produced its first commercial vintage in 1998. One prominent critic described the wine: "Consistent: voluptuous

Top Left: Anne Carver and Denis Sutro have dedicated themselves to creating the finest Napa Valley Petite Sirah from century-old Palisades Vineyard.

Bottom Left: Carver Sutro Palisades Vineyard Petite Sirah.

Facing Page: Palisades Vineyard under a rare blanket of snow. The dramatic summer and winter weather forces the dry-farmed vines to struggle, the result of which is highly concentrated fruit.
Photograph by Denis Sutro

and powerful, yet elegant." "It has been both an inspiring and humbling experience," says Sutro. "To be presented with the chance to create the very best of anything may be a once-in-a-lifetime opportunity."

In addition to continuing the Barberis winemaking legacy, Carver and Sutro have lovingly restored the property's several buildings and garden. The original farmhouse was lifted onto a new foundation and modernized in keeping with its historic character. Former sheds were converted into offices and a guest studio. Visitors are struck by the beauty and tranquility of Palisades Vineyard and the comfort and warmth that Carver Sutro exudes. As a Director of the Land Trust of Napa County, Sutro is also deeply involved in the Valley community. Carver has devoted herself to improving the lives of local children who live in poverty and is very active in the Napa Valley

Top Left: The late Frank Barberis, only son of Palisades Vineyard's founder and homesteader, Domenico Barberis. Frank and his family farmed the vineyard for 90 years.
Photograph courtesy of Carver Sutro Wines

Bottom Left: From the gardens at Palisades Vineyard, looking west to the Mayacamas Mountains.

Facing Page: The ancient vines that create Carver Sutro Petite Sirah demand and receive special attention throughout the year.
Photograph by Ilia Dodd Loomis

Vintners' Association. Both freely admit they have fallen in love with their rocky land, gnarled old vines, and the painstaking and pleasurable process of winemaking.

Chappellet Winery & Vineyard

St. Helena

A modern pioneering family, Donn and Molly Chappellet, along with their six children, arrived in Napa Valley in 1967 and bought 640 acres of land atop Pritchard Hill. "At the time, Pritchard Hill was a magnificent hillside with great vistas and a newly planted vineyard at an elevation reaching 2,000 feet above sea level," says Donn. "It was just what we had been looking for, but it had no winery." Consequently, the Chappellets became the first vintners to establish a winery on Pritchard Hill. Built in the ancient form of a pyramid, the winery rises from the vineyard, mirroring the surrounding peaks. Intended to harmonize with the environment, the building's reddish steel roof echoes the volcanic soils of the hills.

Chappellet Winery, the second new winery in the Napa Valley after Prohibition, was home to high elevation grapes. Suited more to mountain goats than humans, the natural geography of steep slopes, rocky volcanic soil, excellent sun exposure and cooling evening breezes combine to create an ideal place for growing Bordeaux varietal grapes—Cabernet Sauvignon, Merlot, Cabernet Franc, Petit Verdot and Malbec.

For 40 years, the Chappellets have farmed more than 100 acres of vineyards on these dramatic eastern slopes above the hamlet of Rutherford. It took determination and hard work to plant the vines. "Each time a shovel hit the earth it struck a rock," says Molly. "Sometimes the rock was the size of a baseball, and sometimes it was the size of a 10-ton truck."

Top Left: Donn and Molly Chappellet.

Bottom Left: Chappellet Chardonnay and Signature Cabernet Sauvignon on the terrace overlooking Lake Hennessey.
Photograph by Frank Deraf Photography

Facing Page: View of fall vineyard below the terrace.
Photograph by Molly Chappellet

Keeping things in the family, son Cyril handles marketing and sales while son Jon-Mark, who was nine years old when his parents began farming, now guides vineyard and winemaking decisions. Daughter Carissa is in charge of legal affairs and public relations. Three other siblings, Lygia, Dominic and Alexa, serve on the Board of Directors and assist with art, sales and telecommunications, respectively, for Chappellet.

Winemaker since 1990, Phillip Corallo-Titus' goal is to reflect the unique varietal characteristics produced from Pritchard Hill's rocky terroir. The foundation of the Chappellet winemaking program is focused on creating extraordinary age-worthy Cabernet Sauvignon. The Pritchard Hill Estate

Above: Family terrace under the black oak in September.
Photograph by Molly Chappellet

Left: Managing Directors Jon-Mark, Carissa and Cyril.
Photograph by Robb McDonough

Vineyard Cabernet Sauvignon is the crown jewel. "Our mission is to make distinctive mountain Cabernet, knowing the best is yet to come," he says.

The Chappellet family is committed to stewardship of their land and farming in a sustainable manner. "Taking care of the land will allow future generations to farm Pritchard Hill," says David Pirio, Chappellet Vineyard Manager for more than 20 years. One of the first families to consult with the viticulture department at the University of California at Davis regarding sustainable vineyard practices, they experimented early on with releasing beneficial insects into the environment. Finding bug boxes in the family refrigerator

Above: Three generations of Chappellets in the garden above vineyard terraces.

Right: Napa Valley Wine Auction supper on the Chappellet picnic meadow.
Photograph courtesy of Chappellet Winery & Vineyard

was commonplace growing up, according to Carissa, who now travels widely as the winery's "Ambassador at Large."

The acclaimed garden is Molly's creation. Her work in sculpting the land and painting the grounds with flowers, trees and shrubs has earned her artistry recognition as having created one of the most beautiful gardens in America. Ever evolving, the garden is an artful combination of perennial plants and flowers, annual fruits and vegetables, and a variety of olive and fruit trees. A 600-year-old great oak stands on the perimeter, providing a shady, serene tasting venue. The garden also shelters meditative spots with benches for reading and secluded nooks for dining alfresco. Boulders flanking the main entrance symbolize Pritchard Hill. "We have come to love these sculptured boulders and their hidden treasure of trace minerals that our rocky soils impart to the grapes. It's one of the secrets of Pritchard Hill," she says with a smile. "The grandchildren have found their own connection to the earth and Pritchard Hill by climbing the boulders and catching the butterflies, and when they are very still and patient, the butterflies land on their hands. They are learning to be part of nature," she notes admiringly.

Previous Page: Chappellet Vineyard, Lake Hennessey and the Napa Valley from the garden.

Top Left: Interior office of winery.

Bottom Left: Exterior of Chappellet winery.
Photograph by Molly Chappellet

Facing Page: Entrance drive to the Chappellet home in winter. Lavender and rosemary edge the orange, olive and cypress trees.
Photograph by Molly Chappellet

In the winery and across the country, two generations of Chappellets work together: growing grapes, making wine, planning their future and remembering the past. In 2007, Chappellet Winery celebrated its 40th anniversary—a milestone marking four decades of family collaboration. It also honors Donn and Molly, for their vision of a simpler life, raising their family in this idyllic place. Molly reflects, "This is exactly what we wanted for our children when we moved from the city to the country. It was for them to really be involved with the land; for them to understand it, to appreciate it and to love it."

CHAPPELLET

Charles Krug Winery

St. Helena

C harles Krug Winery is a winery in motion. Napa Valley's first winery, founded more than 145 years ago, is today led by the third generation of the Peter Mondavi family. The family is recasting the historic Charles Krug brand by replanting its 850 acres of prime Napa Valley vineyards, converting to organic and sustainable farming practices, restoring the landmark buildings on the Charles Krug estate, and renewing its focus on making top-quality, estate-grown Napa Valley wines.

The Mondavi family acquired the Charles Krug Winery more than 60 years ago. Peter Mondavi Sr., now 93, succeeded his mother as president of Charles Krug in the mid-1970s and still holds that title today. Peter Mondavi's sons, Marc and Peter Jr., have immersed themselves in the family business and today this third generation of proprietors is balancing a healthy respect for tradition with a spirit of innovation that is taking Charles Krug in new directions—both in the vineyards and in the production of Charles Krug wines.

For a family business, maintaining the integrity of the land is more than good business: it is a fundamental belief. Marc and Peter Jr. made a monumental commitment to the family's future when they embarked on a 10-year investment in the vineyard and winery. They are replanting their vineyards with rootstock and varietals matched to the specific soil and climate—the individual terroir—of each property's location. With half of their vineyards now certified organic and more to be certified soon, the Peter Mondavi family is among the Napa Valley's most extensive landowners committed to organic and sustainable viticulture practices.

Top Left: Co-proprietors Marc Mondavi (left) and Peter Mondavi Jr. (right) carry on the winemaking tradition with their father, Peter Mondavi Sr. (center).

Bottom Left: Charles Krug—Peter Mondavi Family Reserve wines express Napa Valley's finest.

Facing Page: The Carriage House, built in 1881, received National Historic Landmark status in 1957.

The conversion to organic farming continues a long record of innovation. Peter Mondavi Sr. pioneered the use of cold fermentation of white wines. He was the first Napa Valley vintner to use authentic French oak barrels for aging wine and among the first to use glass-lined fermenting tanks. That spirit of innovation is evident in recent vintages of Charles Krug wines, which are widely acclaimed as the best in the winery's long history and representative of the state of the art in one of the world's most prestigious winegrowing regions. Dedication to the land and care for the vines translates directly into superior wine in the bottle.

Established in 1861 by Prussian immigrant Charles Krug, the winery was purchased by James Moffitt in 1892. Moffitt held it in proprietorship through Prohibition until 1943, when he sold it to Cesare and Rosa Mondavi. The Mondavis' two sons, Peter and Robert, learned the winemaker's art on the grounds of the Charles Krug estate. Peter Mondavi's own two sons now operate the winery, building on their grandparents' legacy by recasting the Charles Krug brand and restoring the estate's Carriage House and Redwood Cellars, both built by Charles Krug and listed on the National Register of Historical Landmarks.

Left: Slinsen Vineyard, one of 11 vineyards in the Charles Krug—Peter Mondavi Family Vineyard Estates, echoes the family commitment to organic farming practices and gained status as a California certified organic farm in 2006.
Photograph by Charles O'Rear

Facing Page Left: Visitors may enjoy tasting flights from the Napa Valley Portfolio or Reserve Portfolio at the California Redwood tasting bars in the Charles Krug tasting room.

Facing Page Right: Inside the Historic Carriage House an ambience of Old World elegance is enjoyed.

Located immediately north of serene St. Helena, Charles Krug Winery is best known for its Bordeaux-style red blends and New Zealand-style Sauvignon Blanc. The Peter Mondavi family also produces its traditionally crafted Chardonnay, Pinot Noir and Zinfandel with grapes grown on its vineyards in the most prestigious Napa Valley appellations, including Yountville, Carneros, Howell Mountain and St. Helena.

Chateau Montelena Winery

Calistoga

C hateau Montelena is a regal stone castle carved into the hillside at the base of Mount Saint Helena, two miles north of Calistoga at the north end of Napa Valley. Established in 1882, it is an ode to satisfied dreams.

Jim Barrett, long-time owner of the Chateau, states his simple, yet unbending philosophy: "Make the best. Period." He defined the style when he made his first wine in 1972—fruit first, balanced by an underlying structure of natural acidity. Envisioning a First Growth Bordeaux house in Napa Valley, he inspired the modern-day renaissance of Chateau Montelena Winery. Under his leadership, the vineyard was cleared and replanted and the winery outfitted with modern winemaking equipment. He then assembled a team to oversee the vineyard and winemaking.

Just four years later, Chateau Montelena made history in 1976, putting California at the forefront of the wine world. In Paris, the leaders of the French wine and food establishment gathered for a grand tasting at the Inter-Continental Hotel to taste four white Burgundies against six California Chardonnays. When they totaled the scores, the French judges were convinced the top-ranking white wine was French. In fact, they had selected Chateau Montelena's 1973 Chardonnay. The earthshaking results of the competition, still referred to as the "Judgment of Paris," rated an article in *TIME Magazine* and forever changed the status of Chateau Montelena and California wines.

Top Left: Bo Barrett, winemaker, and his father, Jim Barrett, Chateau Montelena Winery owner since 1972. *Photograph courtesy of Chateau Montelena Winery*

Bottom Left: Wine aging in French oak in Chateau Montelena's caves, completed at the end of the 20th century, which can store up to 2,000 barrels.

Facing Page: A frontal view of Chateau Montelena, whose stone façade has not changed since it was constructed in the 1880s.

The wines, made since 1982 by Jim's son, Bo, are created to be accessible and age well. "At Chateau Montelena, we regard winegrowing as one continuous process," he says. Grapes for the Montelena Estate Cabernet Sauvignon are grown on the property adjacent to the winery. The diversity of soils and slopes results in aromatic, rich and full-bodied Cabernet Sauvignon, characterized by the earthy-berry flavor that defines the Montelena Estate.

Chateau Montelena's winemaking history began in the late 1800s when entrepreneur Alfred L. Tubbs, bought the 254-acre parcel after determining the well-drained, stony and loose soils would be perfect for vineyards. Within 10 years, Tubbs had planted his vines, built his Chateau, and imported a French-born winemaker. His dreams for Chateau Montelena had come to fruition; by 1896, his was the seventh largest winery in Napa Valley.

In 1958, the Chateau passed into the hands of Yort and Jeanie Frank, who were looking for a peaceful spot to retire. Yort dreamed of the Chinese gardens of his homeland and planted the overgrown estate in that style, even excavating a lake. Worthy of a visit, Jade Lake has a dreamlike quality. The pavilions and islands, connected to the mainland by crooked foot bridges, rise like

Top Left: A pavilion perched atop one of the two islands in the middle of Jade Lake is situated between the Chateau and the Montelena Estate Vineyards.

Bottom Left: The welcoming entrance to Chateau Montelena takes visitors directly into the Chateau, built right into the hillside behind it.

Facing Page: The historic tasting room inside Chateau Montelena, with an original stone wall serving as backdrop, is where wines are offered daily to the general public.

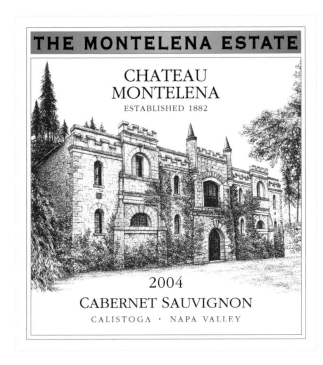

sentinels over still waters that are home to fish and swans and other wildlife. It is considered to be one of the most peaceful and beautiful sanctuaries in Napa Valley.

Experience the wines and the Estate's 125-year history firsthand. the tasting room is located on the top floor of the Chateau where the hospitality is presented with a friendly and lighthearted touch.

Clos Pegase

Calistoga

L ike the mythical flying horse that is its namesake, Clos Pegase Winery inspires visitors to unfurl their own wings, beginning a journey filled with art and wine. This unique experience is the essence of Clos Pegase, where divergent influences such as art, science, myth and reality have been blended, like its fine wines, to stir senses beyond the palate.

Jan Shrem, owner of Clos Pegase, is a former publisher who had long desired to make wine. He attended classes at the University of Bordeaux and UC Davis and purchased a vineyard in Napa Valley in 1983. The tale of Clos Pegase began in the mid-1980s when Shrem fulfilled his dream of building a winery, caves and a cave theater off the rocky knoll rising from his vineyard with a residence at the top. It was to be an anchor for the winemaking and a showcase for the extensive art collection he wished to share with visitors. Holding a contest sponsored by SFMOMA that attracted 96 architects, Shrem was ultimately rewarded with a plan by architect Michael Graves that fit his vision of a *Temple to Wine and Art* that could be visited by anyone who wanted to enjoy works inspired by the muses.

"In architecture, as in our wines," reflects Shrem, "I believe we have achieved balance, harmony and symmetry in the classical Greek sense, avoiding the baroque concepts of high oak, high alcohol and high extract to create food-friendly wines of quiet elegance." He works closely with winemaker Shaun Richardson to make varietals that—first and foremost—enhance a meal. Producing only estate-grown wines from their 450-acre estate, at Clos Pegase, winemaking, like everything else, is approached artistically.

Top Left: Jan Shrem, founder and land proprietor of Clos Pegase, in the winery's courtyard.

Bottom Left: Courtyard at Clos Pegase looking towards Minoan Columns and Henry Moore's *Mother Earth.*

Facing Page: Entrance to the Clos Pegase visitors center. *Bodicea* by British sculptor Tony Cragg in the foreground.

Considered an art form, the Hommage wines are stringently selected reserve wines that are bottle aged for three years before release and have a different label reproducing one of the collection's works of art (Kandinsky, Miro, Klee and others). These are the best Cabernet Sauvignon blends and Chardonnay that the cellar has to offer. Less than four percent of the Chardonnay and 10 percent of the Cabernet is selected for the reserve program each year. "Keeping the amount of Hommage we vinify to a minimum, we achieve the two most important goals of any reserve program," said Shrem. "First, the quality of our regular bottlings is preserved, as the amounts reserved are negligible; and second, the resulting Hommage is a very rich and special expression." Arresting and unique from year to year, bottles of the Hommage bear labels featuring works of art from Shrem's extensive collection.

The Red Hommage and the winery's Napa Valley Cabernet Sauvignon are made from the Cabernet Sauvignon grown in the winery's Palisades Vineyard in Calistoga and Graveyard Hill in Carneros. Shrem is committed to doing whatever it takes to develop their potential.

Above: Entrance to Clos Pegase Winery, designed by Michael Graves.

Left: Reserve Room of the Clos Pegase visitors center featuring important original works of art, including *Wrecking Ball* by American artist Michael Scranton.

Facing Page: A bacchi scene by the great Renaissance Master Mantegna appears behind the counter in the visitors center. Note the two satyrs, attendants of Bacchus, on the extreme right, one drinking from a wine horn and the other from a wine bowl. Actual originals of wine horns and a Roman Empire wine bowl (both around 2000 years old) are on display at Clos Pegase.

"I have owned these vineyards for more than 15 years and believe now is the time to focus our energy on nurturing the vines to make even more exceptional Cabernet Sauvignon."

The dedication shown to art at Clos Pegase—be it in solid or liquid form—truly is a feather in Pegasus' wing.

Corison Winery

St. Helena

I n the early morning, when the mists over Napa Valley still conceal the many edifices to winemaking success and the vague purr of tractors is faint, the Corison Estate is evocative of the early part of the 19th century. A modest notion by Napa Valley standards, the winery cum barn belongs to a time when agriculture was a key part of all communities.

In 1995, Cathy Corison and her husband, William Martin, found this vineyard estate to provide a haven for their family and her wines. Like the Victorian farmhouse that had graced the property for a century, Cathy wanted her winery to look like it belonged there. Her husband, William Martin, a winery Renaissance man and the descendent of generations of barn builders, took on the winery project himself. He photographed and studied barn styles from all over the country, built models and designed a barn reminiscent of the Victorian era, with gray walls and white trimmed windows that frame scenic views of the vineyards. "The barn style is symbolic of the agricultural product made inside," he says, referring to the estate-grown Cabernet Sauvignon that Cathy has made her life's work. The winery also serves the younger members of the family. A platform, at one end of the top floor, serves as a theater for their daughters' elementary school productions.

More than three decades ago, Cathy enrolled in a college wine appreciation class on a whim. "Wine just grabbed me and ran," she says. When she applied for her first job,

Top Left: Set against a backdrop of vibrant fall foliage, bins of Cabernet Sauvignon grapes are ready to crush.
Photograph by Cathy Corison

Center Left: Cathy Corison, winemaker and proprietor, tastes Kronos Vineyard Cabernet Sauvignon.

Bottom Left: Spring storm in Kronos Vineyard.
Photograph by Cathy Corison

Facing Page: Bud break in the vineyard.

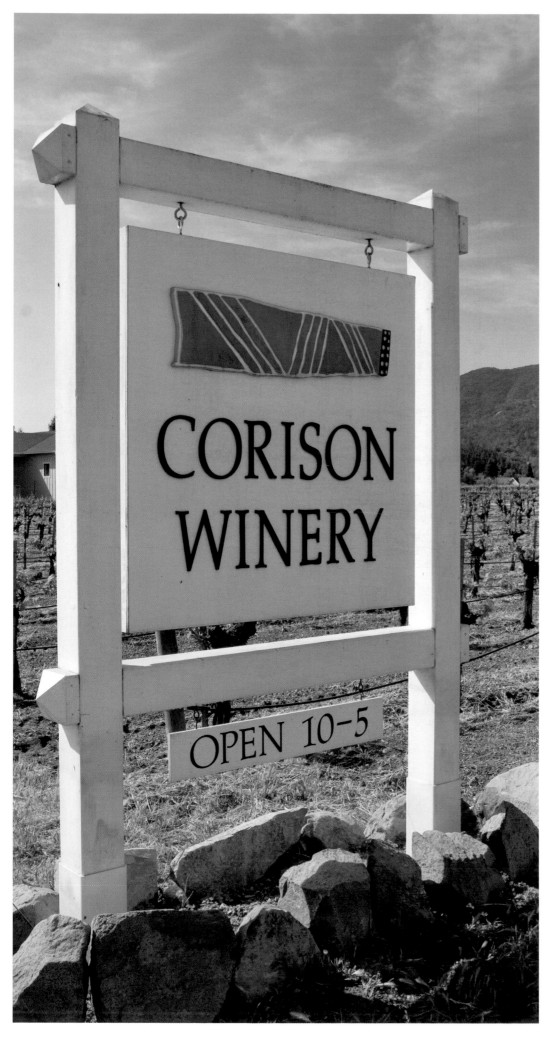

an internship at Freemark Abbey, the winemaker was not sure she could handle the physical challenges of the job. "I looked like a 90-pound weakling, but I went to the winery, and hooked up their monster hoses—and I pumped wine around. We both decided I could do the work, so he hired me." She knew she had the passion and commitment to make a world-class Cabernet Sauvignon. In 1987, Cathy produced her first Corison wine, "There was a wine inside me that needed to be made," she says. "It is my job to let the vineyards speak."

The Corison Estate boasts eight acres of organically farmed Cabernet Sauvignon. Cathy is proud of this 35-year-old vineyard that produces the fruit for her Kronos Vineyard Cabernet Sauvignon. Salvador Marron, Corison's Cellar Master and Vineyard Foreman, shares Cathy's belief that the vines are singularly important. "In the six years that I have worked at Corison,

Left: Welcome to Corison Winery!

Facing Page Left: Morning light in the fermentation room.

Facing Page Right: Power and elegance in a bottle.

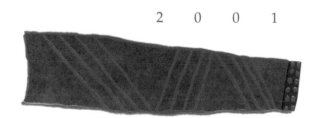

2 0 0 1

CORISON

KRONOS VINEYARD

NAPA VALLEY

CABERNET
SAUVIGNON

I have come to know each single vine like the back of my hand—it is my job to care for these vines as if they were my children," he says. "We're farmers first," agrees Cathy.

At the end of the day, it is family and the land that brings joy to those at Corison. Well, that, and Salvador's rich baritone rolling across the vineyards as he sings to his vines.

Cosentino Winery

Yountville

Mitch Cosentino says he doesn't eat just one type of food, so why should he only make one type of wine? He doesn't. Cosentino Winery is recognized for hand crafting more than 30 ultra-premium, limited-production wines using over 15 grape varieties. With this untraditional approach to varietal offerings, Cosentino believes in the "best blend theory"—source the best fruit, make each lot individually and then find the best blend combination without regard to quantity to determine the final wine.

Cosentino is known for making a wide selection of small lots that are available only at the winery. His exceptional talent for identifying fruit sources and determining blends is self evident in Cosentino wine varietals from Cabernet Sauvignon, Zinfandel, Pinot Noir, Merlot, Chardonnay, Sauvignon Blanc and Pinot Grigio, to less widespread notables like Nebbiolo, Sangiovese, Semillon, Dolcetto, Cabernet Franc and Gewurztraminer. Blends such as the CigarZin, Med Red, The Poet and M. Coz Red Meritage are further testament to the expansive winemaking approach at Cosentino Winery. The Poet and M.Coz Red Meritage—Bordeaux-inspired blends of Cabernet Sauvignon, Cabernet Franc and Merlot—are the winemaker's personal powerhouses that know no boundaries except availability. In 1989, the Poet became America's first designated and licensed Meritage wine.

In 1995, Cosentino Winery was the first to get label approval for the use of Punch Cap Fermentation—a hands-on, old-world, labor-intensive method of winemaking. In a

Top Left: Founder and Winemaster Mitch Cosentino enjoys spending time in the cellar because that is where the magic happens.

Bottom Left: Bud break at Cosentino's Oakville Estate Vineyard signals the close of winter.

Facing Page: The winery's entrance is on the west side of Highway 29 between Yountville and Oakville.

world where modern technology often wins out, Cosentino Winery continues to employ this old-world Burgundian winemaking style. It utilizes manual punching, or mixing, of the skins with the juice. The red grapes are hand picked and crushed directly into small, one-ton bins where the fermentation process begins.

Inspired by an artistic approach to winemaking and the natural characteristics of grapes, Mitch Cosentino's driving philosophy, "the art develops the business; the business does not create the art," is immediately evident in the winery itself. He designed the stucco and block building—a cross between French Château and Italian Villa. The Winery, on Highway 29 outside Napa, is "first in and last out" of the famed valley.

The imaginatively elegant tasting room, designed by Southern California artists, Karen and Tony Barone, beckons visitors to taste upon the custom-carved, copper-top bar dressed with a wood appliqué façade. Sculptural wooden fins suspended from the ceiling baffle sound and create an ethereal design element. The artists' signature concept, reflected in the tasting room's non-linear bar, is that "corners create parties"—corners are more people-friendly. They wanted to create a space that was highly sociable, so instead of staring at the back wall, tasters look at and talk to their partners and other guests. The mauve façade of the bar, adorned with oversized painted figures, is a tongue-in-cheek neo-classical nod to classical art. The Greek God, Atlas, is not carrying the world, but a bunch of grapes.

Above Left: A rare rotary oak fermenter bears Cosentino's signature.

Above Right: Tasting merchandise is housed in this uniquely angled space.

Facing Page: Visitors enjoy the Cosentino experience in the winery's beautiful tasting room.

Cosentino's quest to discover new tastes continues daily on 160 acres of Napa land, 75 of which are farmed to vineyards. As he passionately continues to blend different varietals, the winery's "micro" approach to winemaking remains consistent. Fruit from premium vineyards offers balance and yields true varietal character, ultimately resulting in wines of timeless distinction and elegance.

David Arthur Vineyards

St. Helena

Looking down over Napa Valley from the apex of David Arthur Vineyards, planted at elevations between 1,100 and 1,200 feet above sea level, the vine rows circle and race down the hills merging into a sea of green on the valley floor. Exhilarating, not always predictable, but ending well, it is a metaphor of David Arthur Vineyards. "Never let a little lack of knowledge interfere with a great idea," says founder David Long.

The Longs' family history in Napa Valley began in the 1950s when David's father, Don Long, a butcher in Palo Alto, began steadily investing in land on Pritchard Hill. A businessman, he preferred land as his investment for the future; his vision and commitment led to the acquisition of seven parcels, totaling 1,000 acres.

In the late 1970s, Don suggested planting vineyards on the property. David agreed with enthusiasm. While planting his own vineyard on Pritchard Hill, he worked in the cellars at Chappellet, Phelps and Schramsberg wineries to learn hands-on about making wine. His first vintage was in the early '80s. He made wine in his tractor shed cum barn. In 2007, he completely renovated the building. Now, the neat wood barn—sporting an eye-catching green roof—houses an efficient, modern winery and a separate barrel room.

Referring to his early days as the "wild west of winemaking," he admitted to making a few errors as he learned the business. One was planting Chardonnay vines because the variety was in vogue. However, in the late 1980s, David grafted his 40-acre vineyard to the red Bordeaux varieties that thrive on Pritchard Hill.

Top Left: Vintners David Arthur Long and his daughter, Gretchen Long.

Bottom Left: David Arthur Vineyards is known for its bold estate red wines.

Facing Page: Originally intended as a barn to house farming equipment, the winery at David Arthur was completely remodeled in 2007.

The soils and climate of Pritchard Hill, above the famous Rutherford Bench, are striking. Hardy grapevines twine their roots through red-stained soil full of jagged rocks. The rough, rocky, iron-rich soil stresses the vines, limiting grape production to bunches of little berries that, though tiny, grant big, concentrated flavors to the wines.

David's daughter, Gretchen, joined David Arthur Vineyards in 2006, after she gained experience in the wine business, first with an importer in Colorado and then managing the retail operation at Robert Mondavi Winery. She works with her father, focusing on sales and marketing. "It's the hardest job I've ever had, but it's also the best," she enthuses. Along with David and Gretchen, David's brother, Bob, and his son, Rob, are also involved with the winery.

The David Arthur Vineyards Elevation 1147 is their premiere wine, made entirely of Cabernet Sauvignon grown in their vineyard block planted at an elevation of 1,147 feet. "This particular block consistently produces great fruit, so we decided to bottle it separately," says David. "The wines are very friendly right from the beginning," adds Gretchen. "Our Cabernet is smooth, sexy and supple with backbone and structure to age."

Top Left: To maximize quality of the grapes and wine, the vines are planted close together and given only enough water to keep them alive. Grapes that are smaller in size, with a low skin-to-juice ratio, are ideal.

Bottom Left: The terrain on Pritchard Hill consists of rough, rocky, red soil.

Facing Page: David Arthur Vineyards is perched high on Pritchard Hill, above the Napa Valley.

The people of David Arthur Vineyards brim with energy and heart, which they pour into the hilltop land that is their legacy. The venture was named after David's two grandfathers—David and Arthur. David's father and mother, Don and Anne, planted the first seed of this small winery by gifting David and his two brothers each 350 acres. "I recognize that I am privileged to have been given the property," David says, "but I have worked hard to make it what it is today."

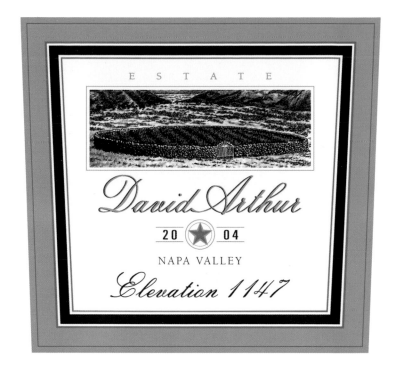

David Fulton
Winery & Vineyards

St. Helena

The David Fulton Winery & Vineyards story touches three centuries; revolving around a dream of making wine that was realized, lost, and rediscovered. Purchased in 1860, the 20-acre vineyard land has remained in the Fulton family and is the oldest, continuously owned family vineyard in California. Today, the winery specializes in producing ultra-premium estate bottled Petite Sirah and in 2009 will begin the release of new wines in tune with the history of the site.

More than 140 years after David Fulton bought land, planted vineyards, built his winery and died young, there is once again winemaking activity on his land. For the first time since 1871, Fulton Mather, great-grandson of the founder, and his wife, Dink, began producing a select amount of Petite Sirah in 1999. They christened the winery—a replica of the old Fulton stone wine cellar—with grapes from the head-trained and dry-farmed "Pet" vineyard of antiquity. Today it is recognized as an old vine variety super site from which a large portion of grapes continues to be sold to highly regarded Napa Valley winemakers.

The vines grow in rocky soil, bearing grapes of concentrated flavor that have made Napa Valley wine famous. Old oak trees gather in clusters on the property, edging the vineyards and lending shade to the restored winery, just as they did to the original before it was destroyed during a violent wind storm in 1973. The new winery, built directly upon the footprint of the old, is simple. The barn-like wood structure rises

Top Left: Richard Mather and Fulton Mather (top), Dink Mather (middle), Jennifer Mather Whitney and Josh Whitney (bottom) and mascot, Tucker, at the farmhouse built in 1864.

Bottom Left: David Fulton 2003 Estate Petite Sirah—simply a taste of Napa Valley history.

Facing Page: The David Fulton Estate Vineyard, a majority of this old vine, dry-farmed crop will be sold to a few highly regarded Napa Valley winemakers.

out of a stone cellar built with rocks from the original building. "It was important to have pieces of the old winery used in the new one," says son and winemaker Richard Mather. "I came here every day after work, gathered the huge, buried stones, dusted them off and moved them for the construction crew to use."

The winery's namesake and founder, David Fulton, started his life in St. Helena in 1852 as a hardworking blacksmith, but he soon became known for his citizenry and pioneering spirit. He was a trustee to the first church built in St. Helena (1857), owner of the town's first saddlery (1858) and founded a winery considered the first built within the town limits (1862). In addition, he was one of two Napa vintners to form a tri-county grape growers association (1869), and he dug the town's first reservoir (1871).

Perhaps his last year was his greatest achievement. Fulton, now an innovative metal worker, had patented his celebrated plow. Nicknamed the "One-Horse Plow," it enabled farmers to work the soil between narrower vine rows—impossible with a two-horse team. In his honor, the current wine label (designed by Mather's daughter, Jennifer) proudly features the Fulton Plow. Sadly, Mr. Fulton died at age 47, leaving us to speculate as to what history might have said of him.

Above Left: Built in the footprint of the old Fulton Wine Cellar is the upper level of the current winery reconstructed in 2002.
Photograph by Lorna Duff

Above Right: Casual gathering of family and friends for dinner in the vineyard.
Photograph by Doug McKechnie

Facing Page: The 2004 Estate Petite Sirah label has a Fulton Plow at the top and his signature below. Below, the newly constructed winery is a replica of Fulton's 1862 Cellar.

Having made the wine that has been in their blood since the mid-1800s, the Mathers are living and expanding the family dream. Following their ancestor's vision, the David Fulton Winery & Vineyards exists again where descendants turn estate grapes into quality wine, worthy of a place in history.

Domaine Chandon

Yountville

Delicate bubbles, fine art and haute cuisine exemplify the Domaine Chandon experience. Domaine Chandon embraced the Napa Valley more than 30 years ago in 1973 when Moët-Chandon sought prime growing regions in the Napa Valley. It was here the French icon wanted to craft an American *méthode champenoise* sparkling wine. They found the perfect site in Yountville to call Domaine Chandon's home. Vineyards were also established in Carneros, virtually an undiscovered area at the time.

Domaine Chandon became the first French-owned sparkling wine venture in the United States. The first sparkling wine was released in 1976, and in 1977 the Visitor Center opened its doors. More than 250 years of sparkling winemaking experience and ancestors who defined innovation helped to form today's Domaine Chandon, which continues the tradition of discovery and passion for great winemaking.

As part of the new American venture, the company set about planting vineyards, which today total approximately 1,000 acres in the Carneros and Yountville appellations. Chandon was one of the first wineries to see the potential of the cool-weather Carneros District, a southern Napa Valley viticultural area once dominated by sheep, but now famed for its fog-loving Pinot Noir and Chardonnay vineyards. The winery farms its vineyards in a sustainable manner, continuously looking for ways to grow the finest fruit while preserving the environment.

Top Left: Crafted with unrelenting passion, étoile Brut is Domaine Chandon's prestige cuvée.

Bottom Left: Superb cuisine is available for lunch and dinner at étoile, Domaine Chandon's fine dining restaurant. *Photograph courtesy of Domaine Chandon*

Facing Page: Thousands of visitors from around the world flock to sample Domaine Chandon's most delectable vintages.

To reflect Chandon's dedication to sparkling wine, food and art, an architecturally artistic winery, featuring a barrel-arch roof, was designed and set amidst expansive landscaping and spring-fed ponds. Gracing the grounds is whimsical art, such as the "mushroom garden" created from river stones. The Art Program at Domaine Chandon celebrates the connections between the artistry of winemaking, the culinary arts and the fine arts.

The winery remains unique in Napa Valley for its four-star restaurant, étoile. The one-of-a-kind interplay between the restaurant chef and winemaker ensures the versatility of food-friendly sparkling wine paired with a variety of dishes, such as Striped Bass on Foie Gras Risotto, or Duck Breast with Montana Huckleberries. At the visitor center, guests can take guided tours or sample sparkling and still wines, along with selected appetizers, in the tasting salon. A range of tours and tastings are offered at an additional fee: Portfolio Selections—a tasting of five wines from each of the wine collections; Ultimate Tour and Tasting—a private tour and tasting of the entire portfolio of sparkling and varietal still wines; and the Epicurean Experience—a private tour with food and wine pairings throughout the tour route.

Marrying the best of French tradition with new-world innovation, the Chandon winemaking team showcases the rich fruit flavors of California's vibrant regional character by using centuries-old Champagne methods and the traditional grape varieties of Pinot Noir, Pinot Meunier and Chardonnay. Blending sparkling wine is a true art form and each Domaine Chandon sparkling cuvée uses as many as 60 unique base wines from 25 vineyard sites. The hero cuvée, the Brut Classic, epitomizes the classic style

Above: This sunny terrace provides the perfect backdrop to enjoy a glass or two of Domaine Chandon's sparkling wine.
Photograph courtesy of Domaine Chandon

Right: Food friendly varietal wines are produced from classic Champagne grapes.
Photograph courtesy of Domaine Chandon

Facing Page Top: This gracious, spring-fed pond, set amidst lush landscaping, sets an elegant tone.
Photograph courtesy of Domaine Chandon

Facing Page Bottom: Whimsical art, such as the "mushroom garden," which is crafted of river stones, celebrates local-artist culture.
Photograph courtesy of Domaine Chandon

established more than a quarter century ago when Chandon brought French Champagne methods to California. Composed of Chardonnay, Pinot Meunier and Pinot Noir, the consistent trademark style of this classic sparkling wine comes from each year blending a percent of Reserve wines from prior harvests.

With a wide range of diverse characteristics, Domaine Chandon's sparkling wines embody its signature house style—harmonious balance, caressing mouth feel and a long, soft, fresh finish.

Left: Blended seamlessly into its site to make a minimal environmental impact, the architecture pays homage to the artistry of winemaking and echoes Domaine Chandon's dedication to the arts.

Facing Page: Serenely nestled into the valley, panoramic vistas are afforded from the vineyard.
Photograph courtesy of Domaine Chandon

Additionally, Chandon has parlayed its experience with the classic sparkling wine varieties of Pinot Noir, Pinot Meunier and Chardonnay into a still wine collection. Visitors are sure to be delighted with the showing of sparkling and still wine, art and fine cuisine. Cheers! A votre santé!

D.R. Stephens Estate

St. Helena

Don Stephens, and his wife, Trish, share a love of wine. In 1996, they purchased a 35-acre vineyard estate on Howell Mountain Road, which they named Oz II. It was the first step towards achieving one of their joint-interests, making a world-class wine in the St. Helena area of Napa Valley. With the expertise of their vineyard manager, Jim Barbour, a highly esteemed viticulturist, they planted the nine-acre Moose Valley Vineyard that same year.

The property included an indigenous olive orchard and the graceful 150-year-old trees stand sentinel throughout the picturesque vineyard. The vines march in uniform rows up to the forested hillside—bright green foliage contrasting with the dark green, almost-black leaves of oak and madrone trees. Intermingled within the vineyard blocks are the silvery grey olive trees, their aged trunks leaning this way and that, balanced by gnarled branches in a twisting grace.

With the help of winemaker Celia Welch Masyczek, the family's first vintage was the 1999 D.R. Stephens Estate Cabernet Sauvignon *Moose Valley Vineyard*, released in 2002. Celia is a winemaking consultant for a limited selection of ultra-premium wineries, and her specialties are Cabernet Sauvignon, Merlot and Chardonnay.

Made from the estate grapes grown in the shallow, well-drained soil, the flagship *Moose Valley Vineyard* Cabernet is an expression of the vineyard. Displaying dark chocolate and blackberry aromas, the wine gains aromatic intensity as it is allowed to breathe.

Top Left: Proprietors Trish, Seana, Justin and Don Stephens.

Bottom Left: D.R. Stephens Estate Cabernet Sauvignon *Moose Valley Vineyard* and Chardonnay *Hudson Vineyard*.

Facing Page: View of the tasting garden and Don and Trish's Tuscan-inspired home.

Cinnamon, anise, bright blueberry and toasted vanilla tones add complexity to both the aromas and flavors, which gently linger on the palate.

In addition to the winery and vineyard, Don is active in his real estate and private equity investment business. He became a lover of wine during his days at Hastings Law School. His son, Justin Hunnicutt Stephens, has followed in his father's vintner footsteps, after first embarking on a successful career in commercial real estate subsequent to graduating from the University of California at Berkeley in 1998.

Justin realized that his true passion was grounded outside of the realm of commercial real estate during a business trip. "I had an epiphany on a flight back from the East," he describes. "It occurred to me that if I were truly passionate about real estate, I would be reading real estate journals. Instead, I was engrossed in articles about winemaking, different

Left: The entrance to the Stephens' estate, "OZ."

varietals and wine regions." As a young boy, Justin spent all his free time with his friends in Napa Valley. Now, as an adult, he learned his family's chosen trade from the ground up working for wineries in the appellation.

"My first job was working as a 'cellar rat' during the 2001 harvest at Miner Family Vineyards," explains Justin. He also worked for other Napa Valley wineries, including Saddleback Cellars, Venge Vineyards and Seavey Vineyards, in various capacities of production, sales and management. He joined the family winery in 2004, acting as general manager. In addition, Justin is also pursuing his own label called Hunnicutt. He released his first vintage of 2001 Hunnicutt Cabernet Sauvignon in 2004. He sources the grapes from vineyards in St. Helena, Rutherford and Spring Mountain district and has currently released his fourth vintage.

Left: Antique French doors open to the welcoming garden.

Facing Page: Cabernet Sauvignon blocks one and five are separated by 150-year-old olive trees, which are also harvested in the fall to produce estate olive oil.

There are more plans for expansion of the D.R. Stephens Estate, including a new vineyard and wine caves that will feature a dining hall and wine library, providing a venue for the large-scale entertaining that Trish and Don enjoy.

·D·R·
STEPHENS
Estate

Fantesca Estate & Winery

St. Helena

Fantesca Estate & Winery is an enterprise fond of women and wit. The unique property was part of Caroline Bale's dowry in her 1860 marriage to Charles Krug, and it has been dedicated to the art of wine for close to 150 years. Fantesca, the winery's namesake, has a distinctive history as well. One of a handful of characters central to the improvisational theater of the 16th-century Commedia dell'Arte, la Fantesca was a plum role for women in the male-dominated Italian theater. Young, clever and ready for intrigue, la Fantesca captivated audiences as a bold and vivacious character. Her smart, sexy wit never failed to steal the heart of Harlequin, instantly recognizable in his colorful costume. The diamond pattern silk screened on every Fantesca bottle evokes the playful spirit of their union.

Duane and Susan Hoff believe winemaking should be taken seriously, but approached with levity. "We want to make the best wine we can, but we want to do it with a smile and a wink," Duane says. The Hoffs were top executives with Best Buy Co., Inc. who became interested in winemaking during their many visits to the Napa Valley. Susan was moved to pursue her MBA in International Business with a specialization in Wine Commerce in an exclusive program based in Bordeaux, France. The launch of Fantesca in 2004 fulfilled the couple's dream of belonging to the Valley in a more permanent way and ensuring that the estate's long winegrowing legacy would continue.

Top Left: The estate-grown Fantesca Cabernet Sauvignon exemplifies the elegantly nuanced wines characteristic of the Spring Mountain district.
Photograph by John McJunkin Photography

Bottom Left: A vintage illustration of a pin-up girl in Harlequin costume captures the feisty, fun spirit of Fantesca.
Illustration courtesy of Fantesca Estate & Winery

Facing Page: A hillside vineyard on the Fantesca Estate nestled between towering pines, live oaks and mountain peaks.
Photograph courtesy of Fantesca Estate & Winery

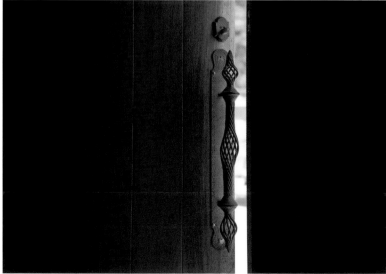

Fantesca sits near the base of Spring Mountain. The Cabernet Sauvignon vineyards tracing the contours of the well-drained, gravelly slope produce small grape clusters of concentrated flavor. The Hoffs use a three-step Le Trieur sorting system at harvest to hand-separate the grapes from the stems and leaves. "It's slow going and only lets us process one and a half tons per hour," Duane says, "but we have the luxury of hand-sorting because we are a small winery." The challenging soils, rugged terrain and meticulous winemaking yield a powerful, concentrated estate-grown Cabernet Sauvignon exhibiting the finesse and rich style that are the hallmarks of the Spring Mountain district.

Right: A rose garden encircling a fountain creates a quiet, cultivated pause in the midst of the dramatic natural beauty of the estate.
Photograph courtesy of Fantesca Estate & Winery

Facing Page Top: The mouth of the Fantesca cave, dug deep into the hillside adjacent to the winery.

Facing Page Bottom Left: The cave is intentionally spacious so the Hoffs can accommodate other winemakers in the region and host community events.
Photograph courtesy of Fantesca Estate & Winery

Facing Page Bottom Right: Huge wooden doors make for a spectacular cave entrance.
Photograph by John Lewis Photography

A bit of the wit that the Hoffs are so fond of is expressed in Fantesca's Fortune Corkies™—corks with an amusing quote or tidbit printed on them. The couple's daughter came up with the idea when she was 10 years old. After a dinner of Chinese take-out, she cracked open her fortune cookie and with it came the brainstorm that started a family tradition. Ten new fortunes are printed on corks every year, including one in the "bad girl" category as a tribute to la Fantesca. That one is always a favorite among women, Susan says. "Women want to be dignified and respected, but they fancy being a little wild, too." Case and point is one cork that read, "Good girls keep diaries, bad girls are too busy!" Each year, Fantesca selects a quote from among those submitted by customers to feature on a Fortune Corkie.™ The contest is open to all, and the lucky winner receives a hand-bottled magnum of Fantesca wine corked with the winning fortune.

Top Left: Fantesca Estate owners Susan and Duane Hoff enjoy good wine and quick wit.

Bottom Left: Fortune Corkies™ have become a Hoff family tradition and a way to share the fun of Fantesca with those who appreciate the wine.
Photograph courtesy of Fantesca Estate & Winery

Facing Page: The Fantesca winery sits in the hollow of a steep hill surrounded by lush growth.
Photograph courtesy of Fantesca Estate & Winery

Just as the winery's namesake encouraged Renaissance audiences to engage with the players on stage, the Hoffs invite wine lovers to share in the Fantesca experience through quarterly events. Hands-on Harvest is one such occasion. Invited guests join the Hoff family as members of the harvest crew, immersed in winery life for a day and rewarded for their labors with spectacular food and wine. "It's a wonderful event," says Duane. "Some people come back every year. We want to keep Fantesca fun."

Gargiulo Vineyards

Oakville

Hidden in plain site, Gargiulo Vineyards is tucked away in Eastern Oakville, one of Napa Valley's and the world's foremost Cabernet Sauvignon growing regions. The 3,500-case winery is committed to producing wine that vividly expresses a sense of place and true varietal character. Owner Jeff Gargiulo and his daughter, April, are leading the charge to create a first-growth California winery.

As a third-generation farmer, becoming a vintner for Jeff Gargiulo was the culmination of a lifetime of agricultural knowledge and a passion for wine. Additionally, Jeff and his wife, Valerie, were mentored by Valerie's aunt and uncle, Barney and Belle Rhodes, iconic figures in the history of Napa Valley. "They had an immeasurable influence on our family becoming part of the Valley," says April. "They made Napa Valley accessible, opening the homes and hillsides to us."

Jeff Gargiulo purchased his first Oakville vineyard, Money Road Ranch, in 1992 and after two years of top to bottom re-engineering, re-planted it in 1994 to Cabernet Sauvignon, Merlot and Sangiovese. Money Road Ranch sits in the heart of Oakville and consists of silt loam earth that enjoys a dry spot on the valley floor due to gentle sloping and a rigorous French drainage system. Crucial to the quality of future wines, the most recent advances in vineyard development were used as well as Jeff's extensive contact base of the world's leading viticulturalists. "Money Road Ranch Cabernet Sauvignon has a dark profile of cocoa, blackberry, black cherry and even licorice. It's a brooding style of wine," says April.

Top Left: Owners Jeff Gargiulo and his daughter, April Gargiulo.

Bottom Left: Most known for single-vineyard estate Cabernets, Gargiulo also produces a Sangiovese called Aprile which means April in Italian.

Facing Page: All original structures on Gargiulo's properties have been re-purposed. Here, an old water tower makes a perfect wine cellar.

Believing that Oakville is one of the most distinctive places to grow Cabernet in the world, in 2000, the family purchased an additional 12 acres at 575 Oakville Crossroad and named it 575 OVX. Situated on the eastern side of Oakville with the area's hallmark red rock soil, it is one of the few vineyards planted on south-facing slopes in the appellation. In the spring of 2001, Gargiulo re-planted 575 OVX to Cabernet Sauvignon, Cabernet Franc and Petit Verdot. "The wines from 575 OVX are powerful Bordeaux-style wines revealing softly perfumed aromas of rose petal and blueberry that lend a feminine even romantic elegance," she describes.

As responsible stewards of these two remarkable properties, Gargiulo Vineyards practices organic and sustainable farming to ensure generations of healthy soil. This includes no-till soil management and deficit irrigation—a method of controlling the vine's growth that results in water conservation and more flavorful fruit. "Our fruit is only as good as our land," says Jeff.

Above: Guests enjoy a glass of wine on the terrace which overlooks the stage for the winery's annual harvest celebration, The Oakville Sessions.
Photograph by Albert Lewis, Mulberry Photography

Right: April Gargiulo on her wedding day at 575 OVX.
Photograph by Albert Lewis, Mulberry Photography

Facing Page Top: Winery guests are welcomed with a glass of Rosé or Pinot Gris and given exclusive access to the winery's grounds.

Facing Page Bottom: Displayed in the winery's tasting room are many of Jeff Gargiulo's handmade guitars from around the world. Guests are encouraged to pick one up and play.

The Gargiulo winery, built above the 575 OVX (Oakville Crossroad) vineyard, was completed in the fall of 2006. Much of the building was constructed from rock excavated from the property. It is a modern gravity-fed winery, built to fit into the landscape. "We repurposed materials and structures to maintain a humble aesthetic, however everything inside the winery is state-of-the-art," April explains. Winemaker Kristof Anderson adds, "Everything is done by hand. Using only gravity to move the wine gives us a greater degree of control, allowing the essence of the grape to shine through."

Designed by St. Helena architect Karen Roberts and interior architect Erin Martin, the winery continues Gargiulo Vineyards' modest farm aesthetic. Inside, the décor of the tasting room is comfortably rustic, but modern. "It definitely holds appeal for the adventuresome, intrepid wine lovers who are not after glitz and surface glamour," says April, who takes pride in introducing Napa Valley visitors to Gargiulo wines and welcoming them to the estate.

The view from the winery's stone patio is serene. Well-ordered vine rows file down the hill away from the winery, meeting the gentle swell of the adjacent hills like calm water meeting shore. Designed by Jonathan Plant, the gardens seamlessly integrate into the surrounding landscape—a lovely spot to visit and relax with a glass of wine. The winery was also a lovely spot to wed. April Gargiulo and her husband, Mitch Lowe, were married at the winery in July 2006.

Above: 575 OVX is one of the few south-facing plantings in Oakville. Notice the tight spacing and north-south vine orientation. These conditions plus 575 OVX's red rocky soil serve to create wines of great distinction.

Facing Page: A lavender bed sits atop the vineyard and—with the help of Oakville's afternoon breeze—perfumes the air.
Photograph by Albert Lewis, Mulberry Photography

Gargiulo Vineyards is a true family endeavor. "Farming is in our blood," says April. "It is who we are as a family—we are committed to producing vineyard-driven wines with world-class distinction."

GARGIULO VINEYARDS
ESTATE GROWN
OAKVILLE, NAPA VALLEY

Girard Winery

St. Helena

High on Napa Valley hillsides, located above a picturesque lake nestled within the valley's rugged crevices, Cabernet Sauvignon is king. It is because of prime vineyard sites such as these that Girard winemaker Marco DiGiulio lets the vineyard terroir determine his selection of grape varieties. At lower altitudes, richer soils are more suitable to growing white grapes such as Sauvignon Blanc and red grapes like Merlot. Girard sources these varieties from valley floor acreage.

For more than three decades, Girard has celebrated its sense of place in the California wine country. With the right grapes from the right locations, this Napa Valley winery offers a line-up that features both power and finesse—the hallmark of great wine. Girard sources its exemplary fruit from several secreted treasures within Napa Valley.

Blue Ridge Vineyard is part of a hidden Napa, invisible to most wine travelers. Only accessible via back roads where real maps and clear signposts are non-existent, the vineyard supports nine acres of gnarly, old Zinfandel vines clinging to a mountain promontory. Higher than any other vineyard in the region, it overlooks the Sierras to the east and San Francisco to the south. Red, rocky soils provide the classic terrain of the finest Napa Valley growing sites.

Much closer to civilization, only a mile north of St. Helena, sits Carpy Field vineyard, farmed by Girard since 1999. Twenty-two acres of alluvial soils extend to the banks of the Napa River, making Merlot and Sauvignon Blanc the long-favored varieties grown in this benchmark vineyard.

Top Left: (left to right) Winery greeter "Duke," estate manager Steve Ross and assistant Winery greeter "Buddy."

Bottom Left: Private tours and tastings at Girard are custom tailored to meet the experience level and needs of each group.

Facing Page: Young Cabernet Sauvignon vines are beginning to show great promise for future vintages.

A splendid outcome of these diverse properties and the mastery of DiGiulio's distinguished winemaking skills is "Artistry." This proprietary blend of five Bordeaux-varietal grapes is from 100-percent Napa Valley fruit, sourced from 12 vineyard sites with a combination of hillside and valley floor terroir. The name, Artistry, was chosen as a tribute to DiGiulio's artistic expression in the winemaking process. "There is something unique about each of our vineyards," remarks DiGiulio. "Each variety brings a different character to the Artistry blend, creating a wine of superior quality. Cabernet Sauvignon brings an intense edge. Merlot adds roundness and finesse. Cabernet Franc offers an enticing herbal note. Malbec serves up pretty cherry-like flavors, and Petit Verdot gives great structure and color."

Everybody at Girard, including four-legged family members, takes great pride in the winemaking venture. Estate manager Steve Ross personally gives private tours, offered only by appointment. Ross is a retired software executive pursuing his life passion—wine. Pat Roney, managing partner/owner, and his wife, Laura, are the proud proprietors of Girard. Roney's taste for wine began in college and led him to management positions at Seagram Wine

Above Left: Winemaking team of Zach Long, Enrico Bertoz and Timothy Milos.

Middle Left: Vintner wife Laura Roney surveying one of the younger Cabernet Sauvignon vineyards.

Bottom Left: Winemaker Marco DiGiulio and vintner Pat Roney.

Facing Page: Century-old vines are the source for Girard's award-winning Petite Sirah.
Photograph by Don Huffman, Huffman Communications

Company and owner of Windsor Vineyards in Windsor, California. When Roney moved into the realm of Girard winery owner, his initial goal was to find a winemaker whose style of winemaking produced elegant, well-balanced and approachable wines. His search led him to hire DiGiulio. Together, the personalities at Girard continuously strive to follow Roney's credo of producing high quality, value-conscious wines. Girard wines reflect the winery's people, vineyard sources and dedication to winemaking.

Girard
NAPA VALLEY

Grgich Hills Estate

Rutherford

G rgich Hills Estate founder and owner Miljenko "Mike" Grgich has been making world-renowned wines for more than 40 years. From a young age, Grgich committed his life to making fine wines and has succeeded through perseverance, talent and following his guiding philosophy, "great wines always begin with exceptional fruit."

Grgich was exposed to the world of wine as a child in his native Croatia. His family had deep roots—owning a winery and vineyard—where his father, grandfather and great-grandfather all made wine. His commitment to making fine California wine took hold when he arrived in Napa Valley in 1958, with only one small suitcase, by way of escape from Communist rule in Yugoslavia (now Croatia) through West Germany and Canada, finally reaching his dream destination of California. It was the beginning of a flourishing career as an internationally recognized winemaker and industry leader.

In 1976, Grgich catapulted to the forefront of California winemaking after a Chardonnay he crafted for Chateau Montelena surpassed the most elite wines of France in a now-famous "Paris Tasting." When a panel of eminent French judges blind-tasted the best Burgundies of France and a small sampling of upstart Chardonnay's from Napa Valley, the 1973 Chateau Montelena Chardonnay was picked as the best white at the tasting, beating the best of France. "For years, everybody in the world believed only the French soils could produce great wines," Grgich explains. "We shattered that myth." It was an event that astonished the wine world, propelled Napa Valley to the forefront of eminent wine regions and led Grgich to his life-long dream of starting his own winery.

Top Left: Fall colors in Grgich Hill's organic and biodynamically grown vineyard in American Canyon.
Photograph by James Rigler

Bottom Left: An image of winemaker Mike Grgich overlooks the VIP tasting room.

Facing Page: The front of Grgich Hills Estate is framed by olive trees on Highway 29.

In 1977, Grgich became partners with Austin Hills of Hills Bros. Coffee family and created Grgich Hills in Rutherford, Napa Valley. Soon after, Grgich claimed another victory in "The Great Chicago Showdown," where 221 Chardonnays competed in the largest blind tasting ever held of single varietal wines. The Grgich Hills 1977 Chardonnay received first place and Grgich became known as the "King of Chardonnay."

Grgich continues to run his winery, forever jaunty in his trademark blue beret, with his daughter, Violet, and nephew, Ivo Jeramaz. They have elected to keep it small and family-owned, focusing on their biodynamic vineyards and crafting select wines. Maintaining the family commitment to the environment, the winery is a fully solar-powered operation. Most significantly, all of Grgich Hills Estate's 366 acres are organic and farmed biodynamically, making Grgich Hills the country's largest biodynamic winegrower.

Biodynamic farming is a commitment and agricultural philosophy incorporating all elements of organic farming—no artificial pesticides, fertilizers or fungicides. Additionally, it treats the soil as a living organism and works to bring the grapevine

Top Left: Mike Grgich started Grgich Hills in 1977 with Austin Hills. Today, Mike's daughter, Violet, works with him to manage the winery.

Bottom Left: Part of a working winery, the Grgich Hills tasting room allows visitors to watch the cellar crew practice their craft.

Facing Page: Miljenko's Vineyard in Calistoga is named for Miljenko "Mike" Grgich.
Photograph by James Rigler

GRGICH HILLS
ESTATE

NAPA VALLEY

and Earth into balance through natural mineral and animal-derived preparations, while following the natural rhythms of Earth.

Grgich has also founded a winery in Croatia, producing wines from the Zinfandel grape—whose origins he helped trace to Croatia. Today, Grgich Hills Estate retains its excellence in crafting exemplary Chardonnay, while complementing the winery's portfolio with Fumé Blanc, Zinfandel, Cabernet Sauvignon, Merlot and a dessert wine. As Grgich explains, "There is no sure-proof scientific formula for making great wines. You make wine with your heart. You have to pour your heart and love into the wine."

The two visionaries behind HALL Wines each have striking achievements and passions involving business, wine and art—qualities evident in both the HALL Rutherford and HALL St. Helena properties. Kathryn Hall has been involved in the wine business since 1972, as she and her family are long-time grape growers in Mendocino County. An attorney by training and practice, Kathryn is a successful business executive, community activist and mother who served as United States Ambassador to Austria from 1997 to 2001. Continuing in her family's tradition, she plays a hands-on role, alongside her husband, in the management of both HALL winemaking facilities.

Craig Hall is founder and chairman of the Dallas-based Hall Financial Group; today one of the nation's most successful real estate management and investment companies. He is a life-long entrepreneur and author of four books on business. Craig and Kathryn have an extensive collection of modern art, and Craig has a long history of incorporating art into his commercial ventures.

The Halls' inspiration is to showcase fine wines alongside expressive art and masterful architecture, providing a truly memorable wine tasting experience. HALL Rutherford, housing the Halls' home next to their state-of-the-art winery in the hills of Rutherford, is dedicated to crafting single-vineyard and limited-production wines. Completed in 2005, the winery offers a sweeping view of Napa Valley. Contemporary sculpture harmonizes with serene garden and vineyard environs. An expansive terrace, complete with outdoor kitchen, flanks the sunny tasting salons of the winery's top floor. Appointed with fine art

Top Left: Craig and Kathryn Hall taste their latest releases in the salon of HALL Rutherford.

Bottom Left: The winery salon is appointed with fine art and Riedel crystal, offering an intimate interior and spectacular view of Napa Valley.

Facing Page: The lower level of the winery is dedicated to the production of HALL's single-vineyard and small-lot wines and includes 14,000 square feet of caves.

and stunning furnishings, the venue welcomes guests with an elegant yet intimate air.

The lower level of the winery is a network of high-tech caves and a technologically advanced, small-lot winemaking facility. The 14,000 square feet of caves were designed and hand-built by Friedrich Gruber of Gutenstein, Austria, finished with handmade Austrian brick and limestone. The brick dates from the Habsburg Empire and bears the stamp of the monarchy. Deep inside resides a dazzling reception area for private tastings and entertaining. The room's spectacular chandelier, designed by Donald Lipski and Jonquil LeMaster, is dressed in hundreds of Swarovski crystals and is exceeded in size only by a similar one that graces New York City's Grand Central Station.

The legendary Sacrashe vineyard undulates to the east of the winery. The Halls own 3,300 acres of Napa Valley and Alexander Valley property, 461 of which are planted to vines. Every HALL vineyard is organically farmed and devoted to Bordeaux grape varietals: Cabernet Sauvignon, Merlot, Cabernet Franc and Sauvignon Blanc. "Great winemaking begins in the vineyard," Kathryn Hall explains. "You must be meticulous with your land, relentless with your cultivation. Only the finest fruit can be transformed into truly remarkable wine."

Left: The private tasting room, hidden deep beyond the hand-built caves, offers a sanctuary of historic brick, fine art and rare wines. The room accommodates up to 40 seated guests and is a breathtaking venue for wine tastings.

Kathryn and Craig Hall's commitment to making world-class wines resonates in their St. Helena winery as well. Dating back to 1885, the HALL St. Helena property is undergoing a phenomenal transformation to be complete in 2009. The Halls have collaborated with famed architect Frank Gehry to create an unprecedented winemaking destination that both honors history and celebrates innovation. Gehry believes that "architecture is art." His sculptural approach is best seen in his most famous work, the Guggenheim Museum in Bilbao, Spain. "Gehry's sculptural architecture inspires the senses, is a joy to be around and brings comfort," states Kathryn. "Beautiful structures, like wine, create memories and celebrations."

Top Left: Craig and Kathryn sample their newest wines still aging in French oak barrels in their Rutherford caves.

Middle Left: The winery terrace serves as the perfect al fresco tasting space, complete with outdoor kitchen, myriad seating options, modern sculpture and sweeping Napa Valley views.

Bottom Left: Visitors to the current HALL St. Helena can view models of the Frank Gehry-designed visitor center while witnessing the work in progress. The new Gehry complex opens in 2009.

Facing Page: The legendary Sacrashe vineyard lies between the HALL Rutherford winery and the Halls' home, yielding exceptional Cabernet Sauvignon, Petit Verdot and Cabernet Franc.
Photograph by Andy Katz

As they strive to make extraordinary wines to celebrate life and inspire the senses, Craig and Kathryn Hall understand the interconnectivity of nature, commitment, art and emotion. HALL Rutherford and the HALL St. Helena wineries embody their dream and are ushering it into a beautifully vivid reality.

Heitz Wine Cellars

St. Helena

After nearly half a century, the remarkable legacy of Heitz Wine Cellars continues to flourish. Joe and Alice Heitz founded Heitz Wine Cellars in 1961, when about a dozen wineries existed in Napa Valley. Joe was a pioneering winery owner, and his genius for winemaking was quickly recognized, helping to usher Napa Valley wines onto the world stage.

In 1965, the couple bought the first harvest of Cabernet Sauvignon grapes from a small ranch near Oakville owned by Tom and Martha May. One year later, Joe crafted the first "Martha's Vineyard" Cabernet Sauvignon with fruit exclusively from the Mays' vineyard. The overwhelming acclaim for this wine inspired the two families to add a vineyard-designation to its label—a ground-breaking concept adopted by many over time. In 1976, the Heitz family developed another special bond with Barney and Belle Rhodes, owners of Bella Oaks Vineyard. Both of these treasured relationships continue today, spanning multiple generations.

Today, the winery is managed by the second generation, Kathleen Heitz Myers, president, and David Heitz, winemaker. Heitz Wine Cellars has remained a small, family-owned and operated winery with the goal of retaining the focus on integrity, quality and consistency.

David began crafting Heitz wines rather abruptly during the hallmark 1974 vintage when his father hurt his back right before harvest. David, having graduated from Fresno

Top Left: Alice Heitz continues to bring her passion and enthusiasm to the winery.

Bottom Left: Antique wine bottles from an era gone by.

Facing Page: The beautiful long-standing cellar built in 1898 continues to age fine wines within its stone walls.

State University with a degree in enology only one year before, made the wine from this historical vintage. He has continued to make noteworthy wines ever since.

Kathleen Heitz has been imparting her business skills for more than three decades at Heitz Wine Cellars and is one of a growing number of women who run wineries. Her biology degree obtained from studies in Switzerland and at the University of Oregon has enabled her to become highly skilled at blending the scientific, creative and farming elements of the business with sales. Kathleen's business philosophy deems teamwork an imperative company element, and she works hard to instill a sense of pride among the close-knit group of family members and 17 employees.

Joe and Alice Heitz began their winery with an eight-acre purchase of land farmed to Grignolino grapes, which today surround the recently constructed tasting room on Highway 29 designed by architects Ron and Hanna Nunn, and built by the Galushas.

The Heitz family owns 1,000 acres in Napa Valley, with 370 acres planted to grapes. All of the ranches are farmed in a sustainable manner and approximately half have been certified organic. The 160-acre main ranch in St. Helena is where the winery and family home are located. Purchased in 1964, the property was originally developed as a vineyard and winery in the 1880s. The beautiful old stone cellar built in 1898 has made the transition through time and the Heitz family continues to age fine wines within.

Above: The remarkable farmhouse has served as a gathering place to entertain family and friends for over 40 years.

Facing Page: The winemaking legacy of Joe Heitz lives on at the winery.

Heitz wines are impeccably balanced and elegant, reflecting the true characteristics of each varietal. The winery typically releases Cabernet Sauvignon five years following the vintage date, with the wine spending three and a half of those years in oak. Heitz is known for its use of French Limousin oak barrels—an aromatic oak that imparts desirable qualities to the wine.

The Heitz family has initiated many changes at the winery throughout the years, remaining at the forefront of industry technology. They continue to be considered one of the leading producers in the Napa Valley with a diversified business in making wine and selling grapes. "Our business is thriving today because the Heitz team actively pursues and implements innovative farming and production practices without losing sight of our heritage and signature winemaking traditions," says Kathleen.

Joe and Alice Heitz, as well as David and Kathleen, have put their heart and soul into the winery and have cultivated relationships with some of the finest growers in the Napa Valley. Heitz Wine Cellars continues

Top Left: The original winery is now a newly remodeled sales and tasting room on Highway 29.

Bottom Left: Heitz Wine Cellars recently celebrated its 46th anniversary, founded in 1961 by Joe and Alice Heitz.

Facing Page Left: The winery is now managed by the second generation, siblings Kathleen Heitz Myers and David Heitz, with founder Alice Heitz lending her support.

Facing Page Right: The sales and tasting room offers an intimate setting in which customers can partake in the many Heitz wine offerings.

to produce Cabernet Sauvignon along with other varietals, all from 100-percent Napa Valley grapes. Although Joe passed away in 2000, his memory and passionate enthusiasm for wine is being carried on through founder and ambassador Alice Heitz, along with the Heitz sibling team and their dedicated staff.

Jaffe Estate Wines

St. Helena

Earth. Sky. Wine. The tagline for Jaffe Estate speaks of the things that are important to the Jaffe family, and encapsulates the Jaffe family's passions, lived each day in the midst of a vineyard. On a property where grapevines stand shoulder to shoulder with the only private research-grade observatory in the Napa Valley, owners Gary and Pam Jaffe appreciate that studying the vastness of the heavens keeps their feet firmly planted in the Napa soil. Here, the daily rhythms of child rearing and community building follow nature's lead. Children play in the vineyard; local school kids and their parents study the night skies from the observatory; and the collective, creative effort it takes to produce great Napa wines carries on in full swing.

Natives of Southern California, both Gary and Pam grew up in a very different Los Angeles from today's—one where agriculture still had a strong foothold. As regular visitors to the Napa Valley, they reconnected with that remembered landscape, appreciating both its beauty and its uncomplicated lifestyle. Seeking a place to raise their young twins in closer proximity to the land and the open sky, the Jaffes seized the opportunity when a favorite St. Helena property came on the market. Today, Jaffe Estate is a lush, garden-like property capped with its signature silver-domed observatory.

The diminutive estate occupies a mere four acres at the center of the St. Helena alluvial fan, yet it is primed to produce classic Napa Valley wines with balanced character and great aging potential. The vines are painstakingly hand-tended by Gary and vineyard manager Michael Neal, a leading local authority on soil health. Winemaker David

Top Left: The first Jaffe Estate releases include the 2005 Metamorphosis, an estate-grown Cabernet Sauvignon, and the 2005 Transformation, an estate-grown Cabernet-Merlot blend. The label represents verasion, the ripening process of the wine grapes; it also suggests the cyclical phases of celestial bodies.

Bottom Left: The Jaffe family works, plays and lives together year-round in the vineyard surrounding their Napa Valley home.

Facing Page: The lavender, grapevines and olive trees, typical of wine country, surround a research-grade observatory unique to Jaffe Estate.

DeSante patiently crafts the estate wines in the tradition of great Napa Valley vintages of the past.

The label on a bottle of Jaffe Estate wine speaks to the transformative experience of living in a Napa vineyard. The nine spheres represent the stages of verasion, the slow ripening of grapes from the pale green to the deep indigo of mature fruit. This growth process holds great promise for the Jaffes. Their optimism and sense of awe are shared with all who visit the observatory or enjoy the estate wine.

Jaffe Estate's first releases are aptly named. The 2005 Transformation, an estate-grown Cabernet Sauvignon-Merlot blend, was made available on October 1, 2007. Not coincidentally, that date is Pam and Gary's

Top Left: The "big frog" guarding an entrance to the Jaffe home is typical of the family's lighthearted approach. The whimsical and the celestial are on equal footing here.

Bottom Left: Against the backdrop of the vines as far as the eye can see, this Napa lifesyle is replete with pool and bocce court.

Facing Page: Rows of grapevines marching up to the Jaffe Estate observatory create a neoclassical tableau.
Photograph by Barbara Balik

wedding anniversary. The 2005 Metamorphosis, a traditionally styled Cabernet Sauvignon that benefits from longer barrel aging, will be released in the spring of 2008. "Life is a metamorphosis, a transformation," says Pam. We should all be so lucky to celebrate it with equal grace and passion.

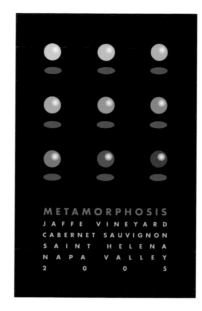

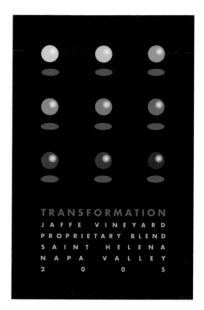

JP Harbison Wines

Napa

"Sold!" Announced the booming voice of the auctioneer. The proud winners at a local children's charity wine auction had just purchased a prime auction lot— a large-format bottle of JP Harbison, etched and hand-painted by Napa Valley artist Pam Morgan.

Joe and Pat Harbison are seasoned bidders on the national wine auction circuit. For more than 30 years they have rarely taken vacations, instead opting to spend long weekends traveling around the country donating and purchasing wine for charity auctions. Joe and Pat, a lawyer and teacher respectively, have always supported auctions that benefit children. As a collector of many legendary wines, Joe would "break in" to their cellar at least 25 times a year, carefully choosing extraordinary wines to donate to upcoming auctions for organizations like the Make-A-Wish Foundation, Cystic Fibrosis Foundation and Sonoma Children's Charities.

After spending more than three decades donating wine from their personal cellar, the Harbisons decided to take the next step. "We had done everything in food and wine, without actually making wine," says Joe. So, in 1998 they produced their first vintage— one barrel of Cabernet Sauvignon that was an exclusive to charity auctions (except for a few prestigious restaurants the Harbisons sold to in order to satisfy wine regulators, who would not grant them a license to make wine if they were only going to give it away to charity). After just six vintages, JP Harbison Cabernet Sauvignon generated more than $2 million for charity.

Top Left: Perfect rootstock for the terroir, matched to French "A" quality clones (budded in September of 2006) and the miraculously emerging vine.

Bottom Left: The nurturing red rocky soil of "Oakville" is home to Screaming Eagle, Dalla Valle, Phelps Backus and Harlan.

Facing Page: The view toward the Mayacama Mountains to the west—spectacular!

A winged griffin on the face of the wine label appears to have magically flown out of a children's fairy tale. It is, in fact, their family crest. Fierce yet majestic, the illustrious griffin is sure to delight adults as they enjoy this wine created expressly to raise money for children's charities. The JP Harbison Cabernet Sauvignon is always rich with dark berry flavors and is crafted to be enjoyed young, but also has the structure to age gracefully for patient connoisseurs.

A true boutique label, in 2006 only six barrels were made, the most in any year so far. The majority of Harbison is made into magnums and double magnums, available only to winning auction bidders. The JP Harbison Cabernet Sauvignon reached cult status almost immediately, due to its exclusivity and exquisite composition made by Gary Brookman, who is also the winemaker for Grace Family Vineyards, Miner Family Vineyards and Clark-Claudon Vineyards.

Soon after becoming vintners, the Harbisons knew they wanted to grow their own grapes. They spent seven years searching for the perfect Napa Valley property. When they finally found their five acres, rich in volcanic soil for perfect grape growing and nestled next to the renowned vineyards of Dalla Valle, Screaming Eagle and Phelps Backus in the prestigious Oakville district, they could hardly believe their good fortune! However, heavy bidding was soon under way. The Harbisons ultimately appealed to the heart, as they have been doing for so many years in their charitable endeavors, by writing a letter to the owners sharing their dream for the future

Top Left: Joe and Pat in their newly planted estate vineyard contiguous to Screaming Eagle.

Bottom Left: One of the majestic oaks that was professionally trimmed by an arborist that will provide shade for the building site amidst the vineyard.

Facing Page: Southwest view toward the Screaming Eagle Ranch.

of the property. The couple that had lived on the land for 50 years responded by awarding the sale of the property to the Harbisons.

Joe and Pat's dream has come full circle, as they continue to help make many other people's dreams come true, all thanks to magical fruit, dedicated proprietors and loyal wine enthusiasts.

JP
HARBISON

2000
NAPA VALLEY
CABERNET SAUVIGNON

ALC. 14.1% BY VOL.

Keenan Winery

St. Helena

High on Spring Mountain, at an elevation of 1,700 feet, the Keenan Winery nestles against the hillside. One vineyard flanks the stone and wood building, the others are planted on the mountainside, flowing over the contours like green ribbons rising from a soil that is reputed to be "as dark as the wines that grow in it." The vineyard and winery are the realization of Robert Keenan's vision of growing grapes and making wine equal to the First Growth vineyards of Bordeaux, France.

Robert developed a passion for wine during college. As a young man, he enjoyed discussing and tasting wine with his wife's family, who were serious collectors. "He was educated about wine at the table," says his son, Michael Keenan. While Robert completed his degree in political science and European history at Stanford University, he was drawn to the concept of an estate winery. His dream of making great wines, with complexity and depth, grew with time. In the early 1970s, after achieving success in the insurance business, he began to search for the ideal location to build his own chateau.

Robert gravitated to the poetic solitude and historic viticulture of Spring Mountain, believing the land would produce his ideal grapes. He found an old stone winery circa 1904 that had been abandoned for years and bought it in 1974, replacing tree stumps and rocks with rows of Cabernet, Chardonnay and Merlot vines; and redesigning and constructing a new stone cellar. "It didn't matter to my dad that the land only offered a dilapidated winery and an empty vineyard," Michael says. "He believed there was promise in the 180 acres."

Top Left: Michael Keenan and "Wine Wife" Jennifer Walker.

Bottom Left: California poppies next to one of the many curving stone walls on the Keenan estate.

Facing Page: Wine-filled oak barrels fill the cellar and age at optimum temperatures and humidity.

After 20 years of success with his well-received Chardonnay, Cabernet and Merlot wines, Robert decided to transition out of the winery, asking his son, Michael, to take over the business. From 1995 to 1998, they replanted the 40 acres. The steep, terraced Chardonnay vineyards were replaced with Cabernet and Merlot vines; and the Chardonnay was repositioned to the flat block in front of the winery. The Cabernet Sauvignon vineyard at the top of the estate, which was originally terraced, was planted in vertical vine rows down the mountain, following the contours of the fall line.

Above: Keenan Winery from across the Chardonnay vineyard. Grapevines were originally planted in this same acreage back in the 1880s.

Left: The stairway leads from Keenan's historic stone cellar up to the tasting room. Rain slickers and hat are ready for a winter downpour.

Facing Page Top: Keenan installed a solar array system that generates Green electricity to power the winery, wells, pumps and nearby residences.

Facing Page Bottom: Large arching doorways allow entrance into Keenan's 100-year-old stone wine cellar. The headstone in this arch is chiseled with the date of the building's construction, 1904.

With the help of the winemaking crew that Michael considers family, the Keenan Winery is serious about its agricultural pursuit to make wine, while working in a vibrant team environment. Michael shares his father's vision, working hard with winemaking consultant Nils Venge, general manager Matt Gardner and cellar master Randy Kewell to make rich, dark, mountain-grown wines. Michael's wife, Jennifer, also known as the "Wine Wife," and Laura March, who oversees winery hospitality, round out the crew.

"My dad knew the vines need to have stress to make great wines; and mountains naturally stress vines," explains Michael. Shallow, rocky mountain soil does not hold much water or nutrients so the vines have to work hard to produce grapes and do not have energy to expend on growing extra foliage. Keenan employs sustainable farming practices. To help the vines out, they plant cover crops in the fall, whose roots hold the precious topsoil in place through the heavy winter rains. The

winery stopped tilling the vineyard years ago, and now simply mulches the cover crop, leaving a protective biomass on top of the mountain soils.

In the charming stone winery, a curving stone staircase leads down to the barrel room. Above, the loft tasting room offers an unencumbered cellar view. Done in beautiful woods, the space, with its trestle table and barrels, gives visitors a multi-sensory taste of the winery experience—it looks and smells of fine wine and history.

Left: Merlot vines in Keenan's "Upper Bowl" vineyard. The vine rows "snake" up the steep hillside slopes.

Facing Page: The dining table in the tasting room is set up for another hearty meal prepared by Michael Keenan.

"My dad knew that the mountain soil and climate were the key to producing the wines he wanted to make. He believed that mountain fruit has a layer of depth and complexity that competes with France's First Growths," says Michael. "We are proud to build upon his legacy."

Keenan

2003
Merlot
Mailbox Vineyard
NAPA VALLEY, SPRING MOUNTAIN DISTRICT

ESTATE BOTTLED BY ROBERT KEENAN WINERY
SPRING MOUNTAIN RD., SAINT HELENA, CALIFORNIA
ALCOHOL 14.3% BY VOLUME

Masked Man Vineyard

Calistoga

A glass of Calix Cellars' Masked Man Syrah is playful on the palate, with alternating bright floral flavors and earthy spices. Winemaker Rudy Zuidema calls it "a porch wine, a beach wine, a wine that is lively with food or graceful alone." Very well-received since its debut vintage in 2003, the wine owes its depth and richness to Masked Man Ranch and Vineyard, the exclusive provider of grapes for Calix's popular Syrah as well as its limited-quantity Masked Man Cabernet Sauvignon.

The estate vineyard is located along the Silverado Trail on the Napa Valley floor. Owned by partners Ron Goldin and Mark Young, Masked Man Ranch is a small property steeped in the energy and enthusiasm both have for fine wine and good food. A southern Californian, Goldin originally came to Napa on vacation from Los Angeles in the early 1980s. Noting the absence of a good pizza restaurant, he opened Checkers in 1987. Young came to the area in 1985, and the two opened their first restaurant together in 1990. Today, the popular Calistoga restaurateurs own wine-country favorites Checkers, Brannan's, Flatiron Grill, Bar Vino and Latitude Island Grill.

"The setting is pure magic," describes Goldin of the picturesque 10-acre Masked Man Ranch and Vineyard. On the market for nearly a year and a half before he and Young bought it in 1992, the property originally housed their herd of Arabian horses. The rocky, clay-rich soil proved difficult for the horses, but piqued the interest of friend and winemaker Zuidema. In 1999, the trio combined resources, sold the horses, and traded pasture for the promise of a vineyard.

Top Left: Masked Man Vineyard owners Ron Goldin (seated) and Mark Young.

Bottom Left: Masked Man Vineyard estate is the exclusive source of grapes for Calix Syrah and very limited amounts of Calix Cabernet Sauvignon.

Facing Page: "The last horse pasture in Napa Valley" is now Masked Man Vineyard. A 300-year-old oak tree shades the house, barn and grounds.

Most of the eight planted acres are in four Syrah clones, each one noted for a distinctive characteristic. When blended, the grapes give a powerful, structured taste and aroma. A few vines are planted in a young, peppery Cabernet Sauvignon.

To fully immerse oneself in the beauty and winemaking passion that envelops Masked Man Ranch and Vineyard, visitors may lease the property's luxuriously equipped long-term vacation villa for stays of a month or more. The private oasis offers stunning views of the Mayacaymus Mountains and surrounding vineyards. Miles of hiking trails offer opportunity to wander away the hours not spent sipping wine on the deck or flagstone terrace. Amenities such as a full kitchen mean visitors can cook up a private dinner—perhaps with heirloom tomatoes grown on the property.

Top Left: Steamer chairs stand guard at the cellar entrance.

Bottom Left: Views of the surrounding vineyards from every vantage point of Masked Man Vineyard estate.

Facing Page: The last remnant of the property's horse ranching past, the water trough was recycled into use as the water feature in the guest house garden.

Masked Man got its start as a ranch but has evolved into a well-respected small vineyard with big promise. "We went from cowboys to grape growers," Young says with a laugh. He and Goldin show that with abundant passion, the most unexpected results can be cultivated.

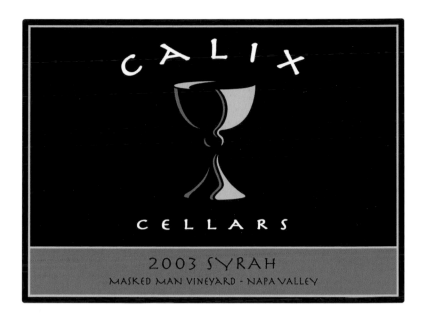

Miner Family Vineyards

Oakville

The dynamic hospitality of the Miner Family embraces all who visit the winery, infusing the tasting room and wines with warmth, energy and enthusiasm. Visitors to the winery are greeted with an open-armed welcome; a theme mirrored by the open-winged logo that graces each bottle. "Our logo of the Winged Sun God pays homage to my family's Assyrian heritage. Assyrians were the first winemakers. The respect I have for the art of winemaking is in my blood," says owner Dave Miner.

Dave and Emily Miner founded Miner Family Vineyards with Dave's Parents, Ed and Norma, in 1998. The story, however, began in 1993 when Dave arrived in Napa Valley at the invitation of his uncle, Bob, who with his wife, Mary, had purchased an 80-acre grape ranch on the Valley's eastern slopes. Dave managed the ranch, and as he farmed, the lifelong appreciation of wine that was developed at his family's dinner table came to fruition—in 1999 he released a vintage under his own label. While Napa Valley fulfilled his dreams of making wine, it also brought him love. Dave met his future wife, Emily, in the mid 1990s. They married the year Miner Family Vineyards opened.

Rising above the Silverado Trail, surrounded by natural landscape, the gleaming white stucco of the Mediterranean-style winery shines like a beacon. Though drawn to Miner Family Vineyards by the wines, visitors will appreciate the personable staff and subtle details that make the winery's hospitality center unique. In the cozy tasting room, the floor is beautifully inlaid with a pattern of vines that lead to the blondewood tasting bar, where samples of the wines are poured into Riedel's hip, stemless crystal tasting

Top Left: Steps lead to Miner's tasting room, which is open daily to the public for tasting and tours by appointment. Visitors will sample a variety of wines produced at this family-run winery from classic Oakville Cabernets and crisp Napa Valley Sauvignon Blanc to Pinot Noir from the renowned Santa Lucia Highlands.

Bottom Left: This modern winemaking facility includes 20,000 square feet of caves built into the hillside that provide the highest quality storage for their wines as they mature in French oak barrels.

Facing Page: Miner Family Winery is tucked against the eastern hills of the Oakville appellation in the heart of the Napa Valley, just off the less-traveled, scenic Silverado Trail.

glasses. Visitors are encouraged to stroll out on the patio, where the view of the vineyards, rolling down to the vine-covered valley floor, is the quintessential Napa Valley panorama. Never strangers at the winery, Dave and Emily Miner, accompanied by their springer spaniel, Ella, stop by the tasting room several times a week. Always a team, the two can be found behind the counter, pouring wine and sharing stories of the wines and winery with visitors.

An extensive labyrinth of caves is a further attraction. Carved from the rock beneath the winery, they offer an ideal climate for barrel-aging wines. Visitors who are interested in touring the caves and tasting Miner's reserve wines are invited to join their special Grand Cru Tasting. This exploration of Miner Family Vineyards' rare wines is held in a special room at the beginning of the caves, comfortably furnished with antique furniture and a grand Persian rug.

Left: Enjoy a bird's eye view from Miner's tasting room deck looking west across the vineyards that stretch out across the valley floor.

Facing Page: Call in advance and make an appointment for the Grand Cru Tasting at Miner. Set in the hillside cave room, this private tasting guides guests through a tasting of Miner's premium wines served alongside a sampling of seasonal delicacies to further enhance this ultimate wine country experience.

One of the wines likely to be discussed in the tasting room is The Oracle, Miner Family Vineyards' signature wine. Winemaker Gary Brookman creates this Bordeaux-style blend of Cabernet, Merlot and Cabernet Franc, from fruit harvested from the Napa Valley's well-known Stagecoach Vineyards. The blend, unique from year to year, is always made from the best that nature has to offer. As The Oracle is inspired by the ancient Greek Oracle at Delphi—the center of prophesy and wisdom—Miner Family Vineyards, shining from its throne above the valley, too, seems to be touched by the gods.

MINER

FAMILY VINEYARDS
NAPA VALLEY

Mumm Napa

Rutherford

Totally pure in its sense of pedigree and place, Mumm Napa brings together the very best of the renowned Napa Valley and celebrated Champagne, France. As uncompromising in quality as they are unpretentious in character, Mumm Napa crafts world-class sparkling wines that offer a luxurious sense of indulgence.

The story of this popular destination, and equally popular sparkling wine, began in 1979 when the legendary French Champagne house of G.H. Mumm began its quest to find the ideal winegrowing area in the United States. A top-secret venture, "Project Lafayette," was awarded to the now celebrated Guy Devaux. Growing up in Champagne, France, Devaux was the ideal choice given his more than 40 years' experience crafting still wines, sparkling wines and luxury Champagnes, spanning across four continents.

Devaux quietly searched the wine country, surreptitiously buying grapes and small lots of wine he considered outstanding. His only rule was to find a *terroir* where he could create wine from the traditional Champagne grape varieties while using only the highest quality *méthode traditionnelle* winemaking process that originated in Champagne over a century ago.

Ultimately, Devaux found his prize in Napa Valley. Mumm Napa was born. He recognized the southern region of the valley offered consistently good fruit in an optimum growing climate, with long hot days and cool nights providing ideal ripeness and balanced acidity in the key varietals of Chardonnay, Pinot Noir and Pinot Meunier. He later broke ground in Rutherford, choosing this winery location to be inviting to millions of visitors.

Top Left: Mumm Napa founder Guy Devaux.
Photograph by Jock McDonald

Bottom Left: Visitor center patio seating.

Facing Page: Visitor center in Rutherford, Napa Valley.

The winery Devaux established and the legacy he passed down is embraced at Mumm Napa today. While Monsieur Devaux passed away in 1995, the winery remains fully dedicated to his pioneering spirit. In his final letter to the winery upon his retirement in 1994, Devaux wrote, "Mumm Napa has been the last, but certainly not the least, of the projects I have been involved in during my career . . . and it will always remain the source of my greatest pride. A votre santé!"

Today, Champagne-born winemaker Ludovic Dervin carries forward the legacy, marrying the exacting fruit and innovation of the Napa Valley along with the traditional Champagne-making methods to craft bright and finely distinctive sparkling wines.

One of the primary sources of high-quality Chardonnay fruit comes from Mumm Napa's own Devaux Vineyard, situated in the cool southern Carneros region of Napa Valley. The vineyard possesses some of the finest, most ancient soils, including the first limestone outcropping found in the area. Limestone, a major component of the soil in France's Champagne region, creates depth and richness in the fruit.

Above: Tour corridor.

Facing Page Top: Visitor center entrance.

Facing Page Bottom: Mumm Napa Fine Art Photography Gallery.

Innovation combines with traditional care in the vineyard. Continuing the long tradition of handcrafted wine, each cluster is carefully selected and transported in small baskets, affectionately known as "Famous Yellow Boxes." Their simple, clever construction keeps the berries from being crushed and in prime condition for the presses. Only the first, most pure pressing goes into the sparkling wines. To ensure character in the style of *méthode traditionnelle*, every bottle is fermented separately. And, equally important, grapes are sourced entirely from Napa Valley.

Mumm Napa DVX, named in memory and tribute to Guy Devaux, is the epitome of the fine portfolio. Each vintage is artfully crafted to capture the fruit-forward characteristics of grapes harvested from the finest plots of Chardonnay and Pinot Noir. It is considered by many to be the quintessential sparkling wine in California.

Mumm Napa is located along the meandering Silverado Trail in Rutherford, Napa Valley. It is one of the most inviting and popular destinations in the valley. The breathtaking winery features a full-service tasting patio, in-depth complimentary winery tours and exceptional Fine Art Photography Gallery that hosts museum-quality exhibits year-round.

Left: Hot air balloon landing next to Mumm Napa.

Facing Page: Making memories on the patio overlooking Napa Valley.

Contemporary casual elegance, luxury quality, heritage, respect for tradition—all in the indulgence of fine sparkling wines. In the spirit of Guy Devaux, Mumm Napa is a magical place where dreams come true and memories are made every sparkling day.

MUMM NAPA

Newton Vineyard

St. Helena

One of the first wineries on Spring Mountain, Newton Vineyard is located in this rugged yet serene appellation located west of St. Helena on the eastern flank of the Mayacamas Range, separating Napa and Sonoma Valleys. Recognizing the potential of Spring Mountain as a prime viticultural region, Dr. Su Hua and Peter Newton established Newton Vineyard in 1977.

True to his British heritage, Peter Newton's dedication to aesthetics and attention to detail are seen in the Newton Vineyard's gardens. Corkscrew-shaped trees stand regal near a gurgling fountain; artistically manicured garden areas grow in intriguing geometric configurations—all overlooking majestic views of hillside vineyards and the valley floor. Dr. Su Hua's influence is reflected in the streamlined Asian architecture including the big red gate, pagodas and lanterns.

The Newton Vineyard wines, winemaking philosophy and meticulousness throughout the winemaking process are the life force of this highly praised mountain estate winery. The single square mile of hillside pioneered by the Newtons is an impressive site, notoriously difficult to farm. This presents challenges for the winegrowing team who must care for a vineyard located on a 30-degree slope at elevations ranging from 500 to 1,600 feet above sea level. Of the 560 acres, 120 are planted to Bordeaux varieties, including Merlot, Cabernet Sauvignon, Cabernet Franc and Petit Verdot—112 separate parcels in all.

Top Left: A sampling of Newton Vineyard wines. The redesigned label features a lone tree, Pino Solo, that can be seen from the valley floor and symbolizes Newton's trailblazing approach to winemaking.

Bottom Left: Newton Vineyard's barrel room is cut into the very hillside that sources the fruit—one example of the winery's philosophy to work in harmony with nature.

Facing Page: The fountain and manicured gardens are a nod to founder Peter Newton's British roots; the Pagoda, Red Gate and other Asian accents on the property reflect the heritage of Su Hua Newton.

Each parcel differs in terms of soil types, sun exposure and individual microclimates. Respect for nature is reflected in the hillside vineyards, interspersed with forested land to preserve the ecosystem of the hillside. Vineyard soils are influenced by ancient volcanic eruptions and are remarkably diverse for such a small area, ranging from loam to clay to rocky. The struggle for nutrients results in low yields and enormously concentrated fruit flavors.

A lone pine tree, over 100 feet tall and visible from many points in Napa Valley, crowns the ridge of the vineyard property. This iconic tree, called Pino Solo, appears on the label of Newton Vineyard wines, symbolizing Newton's trailblazing approach to winemaking. The winery uses techniques based on an old-world style, including natural fermentation and bottling without filtration whenever possible. The grapes are handpicked in small lots and transferred for gentle pressing to the Spring Mountain cellar. Barrel aging takes place in a cave built into the mountain underneath the winery. These purist traditions take more time and care, but the outstanding fruit produced in this mountain vineyard deserves special attention.

Newton Vineyard produces an iconic red Bordeaux blend called The Puzzle. It exemplifies the drive to stand apart. Individual micro blocks on the Spring Mountain estate are picked at the point of optimal flavor development, hand-sorted and vinified separately in the winery—a facility custom-designed to handle very small lots, allowing the winemaker an abundance of options when developing final blends. The lots are tasted rigorously, with only the best worthy of The Puzzle. Changing with each vintage, the final

Top Left: Newton Vineyard's iconic red gate reflects Su Hua Newton's Asian heritage.

Middle Left: The Parterre Garden on Newton Vineyard's Spring Mountain estate offers a view of the hillside vineyards and the town of St. Helena below.

Bottom Left: Newton Vineyard's manicured Parterre Garden provides a beautiful and unique setting high atop Spring Mountain.

Facing Page: Newton Vineyard's hillside vineyard and valley below.

NEWTON
VINEYARD

blend of The Puzzle is determined by the winemaker at assemblage. Another wine identified with the heritage and history of the estate is the unfiltered Chardonnay made from the winery's Carneros vineyard.

Crafting wines of purity, fully expressing the unique terroir of the mountain estate, is the founding mission of Newton Vineyard. Three decades later, the philosophy and dedication remain strong.

Palmaz Vineyards

Napa

It is hard to believe that the history of one of Napa Valley's earliest wineries was all but forgotten. Henry Hagen's award-winning Cedar Knoll Vineyard, in operation from 1881 until Prohibition, sat dormant for nearly 80 years until the Palmaz family breathed new life into the vineyards, the property, and a winemaking tradition that bridges two families and multiple generations.

The inventor of the first commercially successful stent for heart disease, Dr. Julio Palmaz came to the United States from Argentina in the 1970s. During his medical residency at UC Davis, Julio and wife Amalia first visited the Napa Valley and fell in love with its beauty and charm. Despite living and working in Texas for the next 20 years, Julio's weekend passion was wine. He planned his retirement to include winemaking in the Napa Valley. His goal was not to dabble in wine, but to approach it with the same serious, intellectual methodology that characterized his work as a doctor and inventor.

In 1996, Amalia and Julio bought Cedar Knoll and uncovered a treasure trove of history in the basement—original receipts, vineyard sketches, farm equipment and diaries—allowing them to piece back history. In reconstructing the winery, restoring the house, and reviving the vineyards, the Palmaz family has been committed to the integrity and respect of the land and its history.

The circa 1876 main house was lovingly restored as Amalia and Julio's home. The original winery is now a wine library, archiving the Palmaz estate vintages from 2001 to present. Additional buildings house Julio's collection of mid-century prototype racing Porsches and provide residence for the family's two grown children, both of whom are

Top Left: Palmaz Family (from top left, clockwise) Julio, Christian, Amalia and Florencia.

Bottom Left: Palmaz Vineyards Cabernet Sauvignon 2001 vintage with the distinctive drip design labels. *Photograph by Giles Design*

Facing Page: The historic home of Henry Hagen and Cedar Knoll vineyards was built in 1876, restored and today is the private residence of Amalia and Julio Palmaz.

actively involved with the winery. Son Christian and his wife Jessica, who oversee operations and hospitality, respectively, reside in the original gatehouse. Daughter Florencia, who serves as President of National Marketing, resides in a cottage nearby.

From its picturesque slope on Mount George, Palmaz Vineyards includes 18 distinct terroirs. Cabernet Sauvignon is the primary grape planted, with additional parcels of Merlot, Petit Verdot, and Cabernet Franc for blending. Three elevations with varying sun exposure and soil types result in grapes that impart a range of flavors and aromas. "This provides a complete and pure palette for the winemaker's art of blending a refined wine," the Palmaz family describes.

Above: the living room of Amalia and Julio's home features the original decorative ceiling and paneling.

Left: Entrance to the residence lined with the redwood trees planted in the 1880s by Henry Hagen.
Photograph by Robert Cardelino

"We understand that wine is made in the vineyard," explains Florencia. The Palmaz family was committed to creating a completely natural winery in which grapes and wines are handled gently to retain and enhance their structure and flavor, and to ensure better aging potential. An elaborate underground cave of tunnels and domes was carved into Mount George for true gravity-flow winemaking without the need for mechanical pumping of any kind. The engineering marvel includes the world's largest underground soft rock excavation: a fermentation dome 72 feet in diameter and 54 feet in height. The entire winery cave is the equivalent of an 18-story-high building. The multi-tiered cave benefits from the mountain's internal climate, maintaining constant temperature and humidity levels that are ideal for wine, without the need for HVAC systems. Conservation is

Above: The historic winery of Henry Hagen built in 1881. Today it is the family's private wine library. Julio Palmaz built this table seen here from a fallen tree on the property. *Photograph by Robert Cardelino*

Right: The arcade of arches at the entrance of the winery cave on the top level overlooking the Napa Valley.

carefully observed at Palmaz, and the cave features an internal water-treatment plant to recycle all sanitation water for irrigation. Also committed to retaining the natural beauty of its hillside site, Palmaz designed the cave to virtually disappear within the mountain viewshed. Its exposed exterior surface is covered in hand-hewn stone retained from excavation.

The cave was completed in 2007, but Palmaz has been producing wines from the property since 2001. Today the wines are made under the careful hands of winemaker Tina Mitchell and winemaker consultant Mia Klein. Both are focused in the vineyard, crafting wines that retain a natural elegance. Cabernet Sauvignon is "the soul of Palmaz" characterized by depth, complexity and subtle tannins. Gastón Cabernet Sauvignon, named for son Christian Gastón, is a limited-edition 100-percent Cabernet produced only in superb vintages. Florencia Muscat Canelli, named for the Palmaz' daughter, is a light dessert wine also produced in limited quantities. Chardonnay and Johannisburg Riesling complete the offerings of Palmaz vineyards.

Previous Pages: A portion of the Cabernet vineyard at the base of Mount George.

Top Left: Rotating carousel of tanks that are used for fermentation in the main dome of the cave.
Photograph by Robert Cardelino

Bottom Left: Level-two cave of the winery where all the wines are stored in French oak barrels for aging.

Facing Page: Winery tasting room salon with the historic wine press from the late 1880s.

Palmaz Vineyards is passionate about its personal approach; only a family member conducts every tour and tasting. The "extended family" includes full-time vineyard and winery teams rather than temporary labor. Taking a very modern approach to its winemaking, the Palmaz family never loses sight of the rich history of the Napa Valley and their role in preserving the history of the Hagen family and establishing its own legacy for future generations.

Palmaz Vineyards™

Peju Province Winery

Rutherford

Peju Province Winery is an elegant family winery, founded by Tony Peju in 1982. Tony and his wife, Herta, along with their two daughters, Ariana and Lisa, manage the winery's many facets, including three burgeoning wine clubs; a vibrant tasting room; wine and food pairings, wine education classes and hands-on cooking classes with the winery chef; and meticulously landscaped gardens.

The grounds at Peju Province are filled with immaculate landscaping, designed by Tony and maintained by Herta, who can often be seen working in the garden. Amidst the abundant gardens is the sculptural art of Welton Rotz, his large flowing works interpretative of stories and deities of ancient Greek mythology and the magnificent bronze sculptures of Phillip Dizic.

The park-like setting—beautiful compositions of art and nature—overflow with a bounty of colorful flowers that constantly change with the seasons, impeccable lawns and immaculately pruned trees. "Willow Creek," named for the curly willow tree growing next to the koi pond, beckons visitors with its charming footbridge, splashing fountains and meandering footpath. Legend has it the bowl-shaped indentations in the rocks were made by the Wappo Indians who were the original inhabitants of Napa Valley. One of the most stunning landscape elements is on the approach to Peju Province Winery, where a row of towering abstractly pruned sycamore trees greet visitors. The gardens provide a stunning backdrop for the centerpiece of Peju Province—the tasting room.

Top Left: Commissioned by Tony Peju, *Harvest Dance* was sculpted of Carrera marble by Bay area artist Welton Rotz. It depicts a man and a woman celebrating a successful harvest and was unveiled in August of 1993.

Bottom Left: Power and balance pervade the geometric shape in the bronze sculpture *Balance Movement*, which was created by local artist Phillip Dizick. Geometrics can facilitate crop evolvement and regenerate the energy of the soil; they are a stabilizing force that guides and effects the magnetic fields, human form and the environment.

Facing Page: The Peju Tower is breathtaking day and night, but especially stunning at dusk.
Photograph by Rocco Ceselin

Even before purchasing the property, Tony Peju envisioned the French provincial-style 50-foot tower, enclosing 1,600 square feet of tasting room space. Designed by Southern California architect Calvin Straub, the tower's rendering has graced the label of every bottle of Peju estate wine. One of the tallest buildings in Napa Valley, the exterior is made of stucco and stone, with posts and beams salvaged from old midwestern barns. Inside, cultures meet in the Brazilian cherry cabinets, tasting bar and woodwork, floor tiles imported from Turkey, and the hand-carved front door depicting a historical scene from Greek mythology. The centerpiece of the tower is an enormous antique stained-glass window from 1906, depicting the three Greek Graces in a beautiful garden. A weathered verdigris copper roof further enhances the building.

"Peju Province Winery is an expression of how we feel about our wines," says Tony Peju. "To make great wine is to take nature's processes to their maximum and create from them a complete aesthetic experience. Grapes will grow without our help and grape juice will ferment on its own, in unpredictable ways. But, to take those natural processes and steer them to their full potential, that is art whether it be in winemaking, sculpture or gardening."

Top Left: Displayed here is Peju's signature line of whimsically pruned sycamore trees.

Bottom Left: Surrounded by family members Ariana, Tony and Herta, Lisa Peju holds their dog, Leo.

Facing Page Left: The tasting room boasts exquisite materials like Brazilian cherry wood, floor tiles imported from Turkey and stair rails made of copper and steel.

Facing Page Right: Beyond the fountain—carved from a solid piece of Utah-quarried stone—is the front door, above which a marble dedicatory plaque hangs.

In recent years, Tony and Herta's daughters, Lisa and Ariana, have joined the family business. With the sun so plentiful in Napa Valley, Ariana launched the "harvesting of the sun" project by taking the winery solar. Lisa, the eldest, is involved in marketing and attends wine events locally and worldwide. She has become the spokesperson for Peju, appealing to the new upcoming generation of wine consumers. With strong family ties, Peju Province Winery promises a future that is as spectacular as the property itself.

Robert Mondavi Winery

Oakville

The face of the wine landscape in California was forever changed in 1966, when, at age 53, Robert Mondavi established the Robert Mondavi Winery. It was the first major winery built in Napa Valley following the 1933 Repeal of Prohibition. With its Cliff May-designed mission-style architecture, expansive archway and bell tower, it is an enduring landmark honoring California history.

Robert Mondavi's founding goal was to combine European craft and tradition with the latest in American technology, while utilizing education to sell wine. Mr. Mondavi knew the first place to begin was in the vineyard. For the home of his winery, he chose To Kalon (Greek for "the highest beauty"), a historic vineyard property long regarded as one of Napa Valley's finest.

"This vineyard stood head and shoulders above those around it," according to Mr. Mondavi. "It was a vineyard with a distinguished history and a magical nature. Ideal soils, sunlight and rain—to my eye, the vineyard was a treasure. It exuded a feeling that was almost mystical. The place seemed to radiate a sense of calm and harmony. I felt a powerful, almost inexpressible connection to this land. I simply knew it was the place."

Today, extensive replanting projects delve deeper into understanding the terroir of To Kalon, matching soils and rootstocks in pursuit of the fullest expression of this vineyard. New in 2001, the To Kalon Fermentation Cellar was built with oak fermenters and gentle gravity-flow engineering for the creation and barrel aging of reserve, district and vineyard-designated Cabernet Sauvignon wines.

Top Left: Robert and Margrit Mondavi under the Winery's iconic archway.
Photograph courtesy of Robert Mondavi Winery

Bottom Left & Facing Page: Beniamino Bufano's *Bear* sculpture graces the Winery entrance.
Photographs courtesy of Robert Mondavi Winery

"I knew I had to come to Napa Valley and work for Robert Mondavi," remembers current Director of Winemaking Genevieve Janssens. She did come, all the way from France, first working at the Robert Mondavi Winery in 1978. Janssens returned to the winery in 1997 and has been at the helm since, carrying on the legacy of Robert Mondavi. "With our To Kalon Fermentation Cellar finished and the new vineyard projects underway, this is an exciting time for the winery and for me. We continue to follow Robert Mondavi's inspiration, with a holistic philosophy of growing our grapes and making our wines naturally," says Janssens.

Top Left: To Kalon Vineyard's historic I-Block, home to some of the country's oldest Sauvignon Blanc vines.
Photograph courtesy of Robert Mondavi Winery

Bottom Left: A close-up of a 40-year-old head-trained vine.
Photograph courtesy of Robert Mondavi Winery

For decades, the Robert Mondavi Winery has celebrated the pleasures of wine, food and the arts; and provided creative settings for jazz and classical concerts, art exhibits and comprehensive cultural and culinary programs, including the Great Chefs program. The Great Chefs of Robert Mondavi was the first winery culinary program in the United States and has featured such luminaries as Julia Child, Paul Bocuse and Alice Waters. In 1969, the Winery debuted the popular outdoor Summer Music Festival to benefit the Napa Valley Symphony. Over the decades, it has included some of the world's most recognized jazz, R&B and pop artists.

Top Right: The To Kalon Cellar's first-year barrel aging cellar houses young Cabernet Sauvignon Reserve.
Photograph courtesy of Robert Mondavi Winery

Bottom Right: Two of the To Kalon Cellar's 56 oak fermentation tanks.
Photograph courtesy of Robert Mondavi Winery

Educating the American public about wine, food and the arts has always been part of the philosophy behind the Robert Mondavi Winery. With a variety of tours and presentations, the winery has something to offer wine novices and enthusiasts alike. Always pushing forward with new innovations and wine industry firsts, leadership and education continue to be a cornerstone. A dramatic testament to this is TASTE[3]—an annual interdisciplinary gathering of some of the world's most dynamic professionals in wine, food and the arts aimed at continuing the wine education process. TASTE[3] brings together the most compelling writers, thinkers, chefs, winemakers, journalists, authors, artisans and executives as speakers, joining attendees who are every bit as influential and passionate as the speakers themselves.

Top Left: *Welcome Muse* graces the Winery's expansive front lawn to welcome visitors from around the world. *Photograph courtesy of Robert Mondavi Winery*

Facing Page: A stunning Napa Valley sunset in the vineyard. *Photograph courtesy of Robert Mondavi Winery*

An uncompromising perfectionist, Robert Mondavi's life encompasses the belief that if you wish to succeed, "you must listen to yourself, to your own heart and have the courage to go your own way." He lives these words as an inspirational and revolutionary icon in the global wine industry.

ROBERT MONDAVI WINERY

NAPA VALLEY

CABERNET SAUVIGNON

RESERVE

Sabina Vineyards

St. Helena

Susan and David Sabin attended a wine dinner years ago in Napa Valley where the host, a famous local vineyard owner, asked the crowd "How many of you are wine connoisseurs?" The Sabins did not raise their hands. When the host's next question was the tongue-in-cheek "How many of you are wine drinkers?" they gladly responded. The host replied, "The rest of you go home; you two may stay." Today, the couple own Sabina Vineyards and can gladly proclaim they are both. The Sabins, like their wines, are without pretense and full of character.

Always fond of the Napa lifestyle, David and wife Susan purchased their hillside property in 2002 as a creative retirement endeavor. The Sabins replanted their 10-acre vineyard and built a French Burgundy-style winery. They produce limited quantity, estate grown wines to share with family, friends, and anyone interested in making the transition from drinker to connoisseur. The vineyard shares its name with David's mother, Sabina. When the first estate-grown vintage is released in 2008, it will coincide with her 90th birthday.

The family participates in more than name. Daughter Laura designed the bottle label. Drawing inspiration from the family's original business, Sabin China, the S on the label is based on the back stamp that marked each piece of dinnerware, dating back to 1936. The Sabins' son Ryan developed the vineyard's Web site, while daughter Dana helps with marketing. A passionate winemaker and hands-on vineyard manager ensure the process is as dedicated to perfection as the Sabin family.

Top Left: David Sabin enjoys panoramic views from the terrace.

Bottom Left: Arriving at such a finely packaged blend is a family affair.

Facing Page: Hillsides gently fold into one another on Sabina Vineyard's prime property.

Winemaker David DeSante says working with Sabina's grapes is both challenging and exciting. The vineyards are planted with classic Napa Cabernet and a small amount of Cabernet Franc. The older vines produce big, dark, tannic flavors while the younger are soft, perfumed and elegant. DeSante blends and balances to achieve a refined texture and harmony of flavors and aromas. Sixto Moreno assists with winemaking and manages Sabina's vineyards.

Grapes are not the only thing growing on the Sabina property. There are also a veritable Noah's Ark of fruit trees, planted two-by-two; a redwood grove; and a forest of evergreens. The winery is tucked into the center of it all, a truly beautiful and quiet respite. Three magnificent double rows of olive trees, said to have been planted by the Bale family in the 1850s, extend from Sabina Vineyards to Bale Grist Mill State Park. The Sabins have plans to begin producing estate olive oils in 2007.

Top Left: The family room overlooks miles and miles of lush vineyards.

Middle Left: This beautiful tasting room expresses the caliber of Sabina wine.

Bottom Left: A delectable transformation occurs within these walls.

Facing Page: The Sabina Vineyards, home and winery are nestled into the breathtaking landscape.

Gazing out at the historic Mill and the Bale family's legacy of viticulture in the Napa Valley—Caroline Bale is said to have planted the valley's first grapes—Sabina Vineyards takes its place in history and looks ahead to its own bright future.

Schweiger Vineyards & Winery

St. Helena

I n an industry of family-owned wineries, the Schweiger Vineyards family team solidifies this definition with each member actively contributing to their area of expertise and passion; farming, winemaking, sales and hospitality. The legacy began in 1960, when Tony and Theresa Schweiger purchased 53 acres of Spring Mountain property located at an elevation of 2,000 feet, above the fog line, in St. Helena, Napa Valley. The following year, their son, Fred, purchased adjoining property.

Growing up in San Francisco, Fred Schweiger enjoyed spending summers at his parents' cabin on Spring Mountain. He also spent time working on his grandparents' farm. A farmer at heart, Fred always dreamed of planting his family's land to grapes. Clearing for vineyards began in the late 1970s. During the process, old redwood, hand-split grape stakes spaced at consistent intervals were discovered, reconfirming the property had once been a prime viticulture area dating back to the late 1870s. The steep terrain features rich volcanic soils and unique microclimates particularly favorable for Cabernet Sauvignon.

Fred's wife of more than 40 years, Sally Schweiger, is co-owner, bookkeeper, compliance, and hospitality maven for Schweiger Vineyards. Their two children, Andrew and Diana, along with spouses Paula and Andy, respectively, and their children, all work diligently to make this venture a success.

The first vines were planted in 1981, and 1984 ushered in the first harvest. For the first 10 years, the fruit was sold to prestigious local wineries. In 1994, Schweiger Vineyards became a bonded winery and the family began producing wine under their own label

Top Left: A 16th-century quatrefoil surrounds the Schweiger Family Crest stained glass window in the tank room looking out to vineyard views.

Bottom Left: The columns inside the barrel room are architectural works of wonder providing atmospheric lighting with an interesting story. The barrel stacking adds to the Old World cavern feel.

Facing Page: Scenic overlook of Schweiger Vineyards, as seen from Spring Mountain Road, at a 2,000 feet elevation showing vineyard property and family residence with the Napa Valley in the background.

Top: Fred and Sally Schweiger have pioneered the way to work together in the winery business with their children, Andrew and Diana, standing in the garden terrace above the barrel room.

Bottom: A rolling vineyard view of Schweiger's mountain estate surrounding a working windmill.

Top: Since good wines start in the vineyard it is important for Fred to work alongside Samuel and Juan Montanez, the loyal brothers who have worked with the Schweiger Family since 1985.

Bottom: The entry gate from Spring Mountain Road welcomes all to Schweiger Vineyards.

with their son, Andrew, as winemaker. Having earned bachelor's degrees in fermentation science and microbiology with a minor in viticulture from the University of California at Davis, Andrew had also gained experience working at numerous high-end wineries.

All of the wines produced by the Schweigers are estate bottled. They control and own their vineyards, keep the winemaking on site, and guide the wines through every step from grape to glass. All this ensures consistent quality and style from every vintage. To make all of this possible, father and son spend countless hours making sure they can bring in the best quality grapes from their vines. Inside the winery, a blend of traditional winemaking techniques mesh seamlessly with a dash of technology to produce elegant wines that are reflective of both the terroir and the varietals from which the wines are made.

Tours often start in the vineyard as guests arrive at the winery. While viewing old photographs and family history, guests taste white wines upstairs, before moving to the heart of the barrel room. On any given day, Andrew will be downstairs crafting his wines during tastings and is receptive to answering visitors, questions. "This is where things are happening; it's the face of the winery," says daughter Diana Schweiger Isdahl. "Guests really enjoy seeing the inner-workings of the winery. It's a highlight to the tasting experience."

Left: The Schweiger Vineyards wine collection is set for a special tasting in the family residence.

Facing Page: The Schweiger Vineyards winery facility was designed and personally built by the family; tours and tastings are conducted there daily, by appointment.

One of the most popular wines of the tasting lineup that visitors sample is their estate bottled Cabernet Sauvignon. Deep in color with full black fruit aromas and a sensuous mouthfeel, it is a wine that pairs well with most meals. Additionally, the Schweigers produce Sauvignon Blanc, Chardonnay, Merlot and a Cabernet-based Port. Members of the Schweiger wine club, the "Extended Family," also benefit from random moments of uniquely inspired winemaking, where Andrew will create exclusive 70-case lots just for them. The Schweiger family, with all of their warmth and passion also produces the 45 YGB label, which benefits the Tug McGraw Foundation for brain cancer patients and their families.

Sherwin Family Vineyards

St. Helena

Steve and Linda Sherwin were looking for a quieter, more relaxed setting than the Bay Area to raise their three children. A series of weekend visits to the Napa Valley in 1996 uncovered a 30-acre property near the top of Spring Mountain with a beautiful home and serene lake. The real prize was the two acres of mixed old-vine Cabernet Sauvignon, Merlot and Cabernet Franc, originally part of a huge estate producing sought-after grapes in the late 1800s.

With a successful career in construction development behind him and a contractor's hands-on approach, Steve cleared and planted 14 more acres, maintaining the same "field blend" ratio as the original vineyard. The vineyard blocks are named for the Sherwins' three children: Jenny, Lindsey and Matthew. Steve does all the farming, implementing practices required for hillside plantings. The use of cover crops—a blend of natural meadow grasses—is crucial to soil conservation.

Sherwin Family Vineyards released their first wine in 1999, which was from the 1996 vintage. Linda compared her first harvest to an episode of "I Love Lucy," where Lucy, dressed in Tuscan garb, naively thrashes about in a vat of Italian grapes. According to Linda, she had to learn somewhere!

Marked by the firm backbone of Spring Mountain fruit, the Sherwin Family Vineyards Estate Cabernet Sauvignon exhibits the density, concentration and intense flavors of the appellation. "I'm always surprised and thrilled at events when someone tastes our wine and then grabs all their friends to come over to taste it, too," says Linda.

Top Left: Panoramic views are afforded from the winery's garden and side patio.

Middle Left: Linda and Steve Sherwin enjoy sipping wine inside the tasting room.

Bottom Left: The beautiful patio overlooks acres of lush vegetation.

Facing Page: Enveloped by mature trees, the side of the winery is lightly covered with ivy.

Community minded and deeply patriotic, the Sherwins created a very special bottle featuring the American flag after September 11 to benefit the families of those lost in the disaster. "As far as I know, we are the first and only winery in the United States permitted to place the American flag on our bottles for legal sale of alcohol," Steve says. Every year, a limited number of these beautiful Commemorative Etched American Flag bottles are produced, each hand-painted and numbered. Sherwin Family Vineyards continues to donate these bottles to various charitable causes, as well as offering them to customers at the winery. "They are a hit and we're jazzed. Donating the flag bottles to charity is one way we can give back."

The winery and tasting room are as welcoming as the Sherwins. With an indisputable European flair, the tasting room projects the aura of a living room, compelling guests to have another look around—checking for signs indicating that they did not inadvertently wander into the family home. Linda's courtly jesters—one is named King Bravado—preside over the clubby décor, which conjures images of guests relaxing and chatting over a glass of Sherwin Cabernet Sauvignon, favorite dogs snoozing

Top Left: Positioned beside bottles of Estate Cabernet Sauvignon is a limited-edition American flag bottle.

Bottom Left: The Sherwin family: Jen, Steve, Linda, Matt and Lindsey.

Facing Page: Views of the estate vineyard are enjoyed from the winery patio.
Photograph by Steve Sherwin

at their feet. Depending on the season, visitors may relax in front of a hearty blaze crackling in the fireplace or stroll out to the patio for a view that rolls down the vineyard rows into the lake, its central fountain splashing over ducks paddling in the summer sun.

Sherwin Family Vineyards is a place to visit and spend some time—to savor the wine, as well as the lifestyle.

Spottswoode Estate Vineyard & Winery

St. Helena

Spottswoode is a historic family-owned vineyard and winery known for producing classic, refined Cabernet Sauvignon and Sauvignon Blanc. For more than 35 years, the Novak family has honored this estate by maintaining the historic buildings and gardens, replanting and organically farming the vineyards, and restoring the natural environment of adjacent Spring Creek.

In 1972—due to their desire to raise their family in a more rural environment—Mary and Jack Novak purchased the estate, located on the western edge of St. Helena at the base of the Mayacamas Range. Though Jack passed away unexpectedly five years later at the age of 44, Mary made the decision to keep her five children in the Napa Valley and to continue the dream she shared with her husband. Today, two of Mary's daughters, Beth and Lindy, work for the family winery. "As a family, we feel very fortunate to be stewards of such a remarkable piece of land," says Beth.

Organically farmed since 1985, Spottswoode has been certified by the California Certified Organic Farmers since 1990, and continues to employ the latest organic farming techniques. The 40-acre estate is planted primarily to Cabernet Sauvignon grapes. "We aspire to improve the health of the soil and the vines, thereby improving fruit conditions and increasing the flavor concentration of the grapes and wines," says Mary. "The trademark terroir of Spottswoode speaks in each glass of wine." The vines grow in the alluvial, sandy loam soil that allows for superb drainage and natural canopy management, redirecting the vines' energy toward producing fruit instead of foliage. Cover crops, fertigation (applying organic fertilizer), and many other organic farming

Top Left: Built in 1882, the Victorian Estate home is a tribute to Napa Valley's rich history.

Middle Left: Winery owner Mary Novak.
Photograph courtesy of Spottswoode Estate Vineyard & Winery

Bottom Left: The colorful rose garden opens to the fruit orchard and organically farmed Estate Vineyard.

Facing Page: Entrance to the beautiful, historic Spottswoode Estate.
Photograph courtesy of Spottswoode Estate Vineyard & Winery

methods promote a healthy environment for the flora and fauna on the estate. Olive trees and other plants grown in the extensive gardens provide homes for bees and other beneficial insects.

"Our successful effort to restore Spring Creek is an inspiring example of how communities can work together," says Lindy. The progress is tangible. Creek banks that were at risk are now shored up using environmentally friendly techniques, such as woven willow walls or rocks strategically placed under tree roots. Rock weirs, placed in the bottom of the creek, encourage sediment to collect and reestablish the bed, and non-native plants have been replaced with native flora.

The year 2007 marked the 125th anniversary of the Spottswoode Estate, christened by Mrs. Albert Spotts, whose family owned the property from 1910 until 1972. In addition to the elegant Victorian home and formal gardens constructed circa 1882, there are two other historic buildings on the adjacent winery property: a Victorian farmhouse, which serves as the office, and a pre-Prohibition stone cellar used to barrel age the Cabernet Sauvignon. The winery, designed to fit in with the original buildings, was finished in time for the 1999 harvest. Spottswoode also celebrated its 25th anniversary as a winery in 2007—its first vintage was the 1982 Estate Cabernet Sauvignon, made exactly 100 years after the estate was founded.

Top Left: Mary's daughter and winery president, Beth Novak Milliken.
Photograph courtesy of Spottswoode Estate Vineyard & Winery

Bottom Left: The Spottswoode Estate Cabernet Sauvignon aging in the pre-Prohibition stone wine cellar.

Facing Page: Spottswoode is renowned for its exceptional, estate-grown Cabernet Sauvignon.
Photograph courtesy of Spottswoode Estate Vineyard & Winery

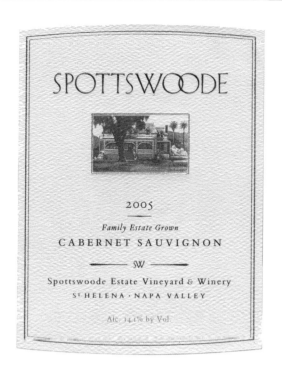

Five generations of families have lived at Spottswoode. Each has left their individual mark on the estate, even through Prohibition and the Depression. As the fifth generation—not through their ancestors, but through their dedication to the land—the Novaks consider themselves bound to the estate. "Our long-term family goal is to keep the property in the family and take the time needed to establish this piece of ground as one of the best vineyards in the world," says Beth.

Spring Mountain Vineyard

St. Helena

Spring Mountain Vineyard galvanized into motion more than a century ago. A history steeped in land-owning pioneers, expansive vineyards, extravagant construction and luscious gardens laid the foundation for the modern-day Spring Mountain Vineyard.

In 1884, Abby Parrott purchased an 800-acre estate northwest of St. Helena. The widow of United States Mexican consul John Parrott, she had her stepson, Tiburcio, develop the ranch. He set about planting vineyards and began tunneling a cave for his wine cellar. The estate gardens were filled with 5,000 olive trees, 1,000 citrus trees and 5,000 roses in 250 different varieties. Tiburcio commissioned a dramatically styled Victorian home, aptly named Miravalle, Spanish for "view of the valley," as it is situated on a rise above St. Helena. He also built a barn of Eastlake architecture and finished the inside with polished wood, ornate cast iron divisions for stalls and iron feed boxes.

Unfortunately, Tiburcio died in 1894 and never saw the winery that was to sit at the entrance to his cave. His stepmother sold the ranch equipment and closed Miravalle. For years, the cave sat, unfinished and unused. In 1974, the Miravalle estate was purchased and a 17,000-square-foot winery was built at the mouth of the original cave. Validating Tiburcio's desire to make world-class claret, a wine from Spring Mountain Vineyard was among a group of Napa wines that bested the greatest French wines in the now famous "Judgment of Paris" wine tasting in 1976.

Top Left: Spring Mountain Vineyard's estate-grown Elivette and Sauvignon Blanc stand ready for tasting on the front porch of the 1885 Villa Miravalle.

Bottom Left: Spring's first flush of roses climb the stately palm trees near the Miravalle vineyard.

Facing Page: The 1885 Villa Miravalle is an elegant venue for tasting wines of the Spring Mountain Vineyard.

The renaissance of Spring Mountain Vineyard began in 1992 by its owner, Jacob E. Safra, whose goal was to make one Bordeaux-styled red wine that captures the quintessential nature of his Napa Valley wine estate. Safra's European heritage is evident everywhere: from his meticulous restoration of vineyards and historic architecture to the lush year-round gardens. With similar goals separated by 100 years, Safra and Parrott share a passion for creating beauty from the land.

Spring Mountain Vineyard was once four separate but contiguous properties, each with its own vineyard, winery and history. Today, it is an 845-acre estate of forest and vineyard on the eastern slopes of Spring Mountain, extending 400 feet above sea level to 1,600 feet at the pinnacle.

Top Left: The winery at Spring Mountain Vineyard, built in 1974, sits against the original hillside cave dating to 1886.

Bottom Left: Original stained glass reflects the sunshine in the Villa Miravalle dining salon where guests sample wines from the estate.

Facing Page: The steep terraces of Spring Mountain Vineyard's Chateau Chevalier were first carved into the hillside and planted to vines in the 1880s. The vineyard consistently yields wines of power and elegance.

The vineyard occupies approximately 226 acres of the estate and is separated into 135 small hillside blocks. Each block has been planted to maximize the unique characteristics of differing microclimates, soil and sun exposure. A substantial portion of the vineyard is planted in meter by meter spacing, using vertical Gobelet, an ancient vine training method. Although it is costly and labor intensive, the resulting grape quality merits the effort.

Every vineyard block is farmed to produce exceptional wines showing power and depth in the mountain fruit, while maintaining balance through gentle winemaking techniques. All wines from Spring Mountain Vineyard are estate-grown and bottled, ensuring consistent wines of power, elegance and longevity. Widely recognized is Elivette, a reserve blend crafted from carefully selected lots of Cabernet Sauvignon, Merlot, Cabernet Franc and Petit Verdot. The vineyard also produces Sauvignon Blanc, Syrah and Pinot Noir.

Tours are available by advance reservation. Visitors to Spring Mountain Vineyard experience a unique sense of place and history through a walking tour of the original 1885 estate, including the winery, caves, vineyards and gardens. The tour finishes with a seated tasting in Villa Miravalle, overlooking the picturesque expanse of Napa Valley. Villa Miravalle, designed by Albert Schroepfer, architect of San Francisco's Orpheum Theater and other well-known Napa Valley landmarks, is a spectacular 8,000-square-foot Victorian with its original 19th-century stained glass windows, exquisite inlaid floors and ornate mouldings.

Above: The original wine cave at Spring Mountain Vineyard where Cabernet Sauvignon and other estate-grown red wines age in French oak barrels.

Facing Page: Small stainless fermenters sit in close proximity to the cave's new French oak barrels where Spring Mountain's estate wines spend many months before they are blended and bottled.

The past is as glorious as the present. Transformation has been the catalyst to merging multiple vineyards and wineries into one stronghold, personified today in Spring Mountain Vineyard.

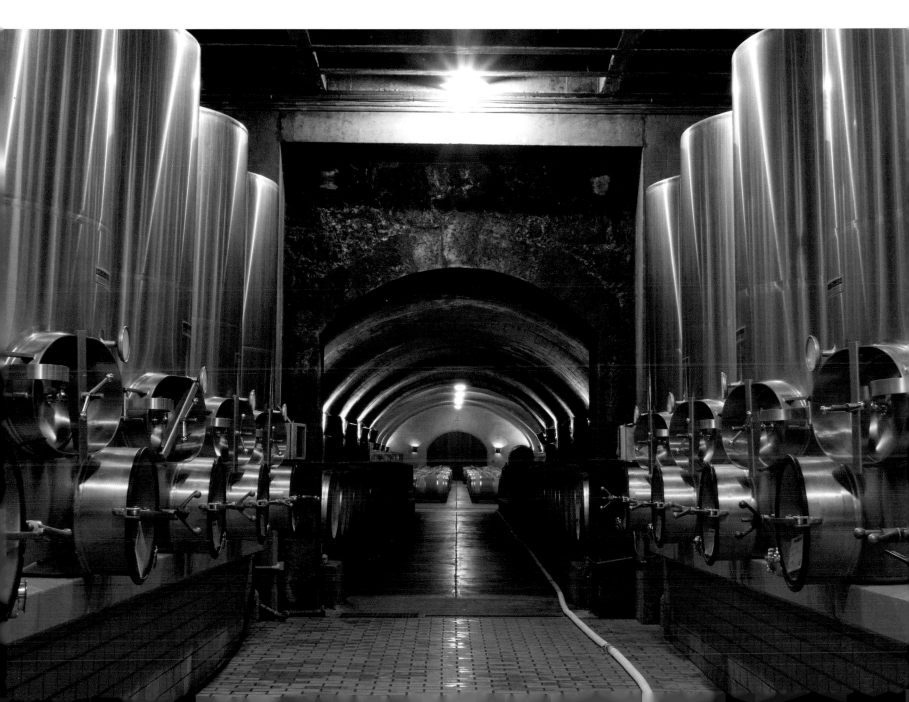

St. Supéry Vineyards & Winery

Rutherford

The graceful, camphor-lined lane entering St. Supéry Winery leads into a wine lover's park. Located in Napa Valley's Rutherford appellation, the welcoming view is of a fully restored Victorian, the historic 1882 Atkinson House, framed by a giant magnolia tree of the same vintage and an ancient, majestic oak encircled by an expanse of velvety green lawn. Further along, a pétanque parc entertains participants and provides interest to the entrance of the winery and visitor center. Nearby, estate vineyards of Cabernet Sauvignon, Merlot and Petit Verdot surround the gardens and winery.

In the foyer, a friendly greeter welcomes guests to the French-owned Skalli family winery, which specializes in Bordeaux varietals, primarily Sauvignon Blanc and Cabernet Sauvignon. Unique and memorable experiences are offered in a relaxed, friendly manner, for the novice to the sophisticated wine connoisseur. On the main floor, a hospitable tasting room—hosted by a group of knowledgeable staff members— offers an array of St. Supéry estate wines and two Meritage blends: Élu and Virtú. Élu is a blend of Cabernet Sauvignon, Merlot, Petit Verdot and Malbec. Virtú exhibits the hallmark St. Supéry Sauvignon Blanc merged with Sémillon.

A self-guided tour from the gallery level gives a bird's-eye view of the winemaking facility, with explanations provided by reader boards at each point of interest. Guided tours are also available. A permanent educational exhibit, complete with visual displays, highlights the winemaking and winegrowing processes. The exhibit includes a dramatic museum-quality replica of a head-trained grape vine with soil and roots, delicately

Top Left: St. Supéry's Smellavision releases aromas commonly found in Sauvignon Blanc and Cabernet Sauvignon such as pink grapefruit and black cherry.
Photograph by Tina Cao

Bottom Left: Make wine the old-fashioned way. St. Supéry's Harvest Adventures include a grape stomp, one of many fun things you can do at the winery.
Photograph by Jeff Hawker

Facing Page: A perennially green tree-lined allée welcomes visitors to St. Supéry.

graced by a perched California quail. The one-of-a-kind Smellavision gives guests a sensory experience of wine aromatics.

Additionally, the adjacent art gallery features seasonal exhibits by local and international artists as well as a magnificent view of the trees and gardens. For the serious enophile, the Divine Wine Room is open on weekends for tasting of St. Supéry Meritage wines, Limited Edition Estate Cabernet Sauvignons, library selections and small-production wines available exclusively at the winery.

The winery is also known for its fun events and seminars. The annual Élu Party is the signature event. Forty teams, of 10-15 people each, are given a selection of components to blend into a Meritage wine. CEO Michaela Rodeno and winemaker Michael Beaulac judge the highly competitive contest, awarding a six-liter bottle of St. Supéry Meritage to the winning team.

In addition to the 35-acre Rutherford estate vineyard, St. Supéry also owns 475 acres of vines planted at Dollarhide ranch, including almost 200 acres of Sauvignon Blanc and an equal amount of Cabernet Sauvignon.

Top Left: Everyone enjoys a glass of Élu, red Meritage, while playing a game of pétanque in the parc.
Photograph by Tina Cao

Bottom Left: The tasting room and wine shop offers several special, exclusive wines available only to visitors and club members.

Facing Page: The historic Atkinson House.

"We have become the leading producer of Sauvignon Blanc in Napa Valley," says Rodeno. "We are very happy to own about 10 percent of all the Sauvignon Blanc planted in Napa Valley." Purchased in 1982 by French wine industry leader Robert Skalli, Dollarhide ranch is a scenic private valley high in the eastern mountains of the Napa Valley AVA. Its seven lakes, diverse soil types, 350-foot changes in elevation, specimen oaks and open meadows made it ideal for grape growing. Today, St. Supéry's Dollarhide ranch is home to Bordeaux varieties planted on steep terraces and rolling hillsides. As Rodeno emphasizes, "We are the followers of our vineyards."

St. Supéry

VINEYARDS & WINERY, NAPA VALLEY, CALIFORNIA

Staglin Family Vineyard

Rutherford

S taglin Family Vineyard was selected as an ideal location to plant Cabernet Sauvignon by the renowned wine pioneer Andre Tchelistcheff, in 1965. Honoring the more than 40-year legacy of their land and vines, the family is committed to conservation. "In the 21 years we've been here—close to this land and vineyard— we realize we are stewards passing through. It's up to us to pass it along in a better condition than when we first arrived on the scene," says Shari Staglin, owner of the property with her husband Garen.

The certified-organic vineyards reflect the sustainable farming practiced here since 1990. The estate, planted mainly to Cabernet Sauvignon and Sangiovese, has a few acres of denser soils where Chardonnay flourishes. Vineyard manager David Abreu employs a natural farming practice, called biodiversity, to keep the vineyards healthy and balanced without pesticides or chemicals.

David added to the property a variety of cross-pollinating plants, including olive trees, clover and lavender, bringing in beehives to aid in the pollination. "Sweet peas, native grasses, vetch and mustard are growing in abundance, and we've spotted increasing numbers of bluebirds, dragonflies and ladybugs, indicators of a healthy environment," says Shari.

Top Left: The Caves' tasting room welcomes guests.

Bottom Left: Spring flowers in the garden behind the house.

Facing Page: *Winged Woman Walking*, sculpted by Stephen DeStaebler, appears on the Staglins' label, inspiring them to keep striding forward.

Harvest is the climax to the winegrowing year. Transferring precious fruit from mother vine to fermentation tank without corrupting the flavor requires care. Crews start before dawn, picking into small boxes while the still-cool temperatures preserve the fruit's flavor balance. Harvested grapes make a short trip to the winery where they are de-stemmed to whole berries and "extreme sorted" by hand, berry by berry, to ensure perfect fruit.

Finished in 2002, the new winery was completed 17 years after the family purchased the property. Like the vineyards, the winery design is all about conservation as it operates on solar power and uses only well water. "We believe that going Green is important and practical," says Garen. Tunneled into the hillside under the vineyards, the facility is completely underground and not one vine or oak tree was displaced. The cool, humid caves house an entire winery, providing an ideal environment for making and storing wine. A regal underground room with chandelier and trestle table for special tastings is at the center; huge windows span the hillside, welcoming light and views of the valley.

Above: Guests at Shari and Garen's home find the loggia a pleasant place to relax.
Photograph by Doug Dunn, BAR Architects

Right: The family enjoys preparing meals in the kitchen.
Photograph by Doug Dunn, BAR Architects

Facing Page Top: Agustin, Dave and vineyard manager David Abreu's crew hand-sort individual Cabernet berries for optimal ripeness.
Photograph by Doug Dunn, BAR Architects

Facing Page Bottom: Now in its 13th year, the Staglins' annual Music Festival for Mental Health has raised almost $35 million for brain disorder research.
Photograph by Andy Berry

The vine rows end at the Staglin lawn, but the vineyards are kept at the forefront, as grapevine-trellised verandas frame views from inside their home. Striking modern sculptures, strategically placed on patios, lawns and throughout the gardens, inspire contemplation as well as humor. It is a lush estate where a stroll through the garden could end as a meditation on fine art.

As the land grants its bounty to them, the Staglin family, in turn, gives generously to charitable organizations. "Our philosophy of 'Great Wines for Great Causes' has developed over the years. We are committed to giving back to the community by using our wine for good deeds," says Garen.

"The most important fundraiser for us is the Music Festival for Mental Health. After our event in 2007, we will have raised funds approaching 35 million dollars," says Garen. With the help of celebrities, scientists and supportive attendees, they raise money for a cause often ignored because it makes people uncomfortable. Garen encourages people to visit the site via a link on the Staglin home page.

Top Left: Each fermenting tank room is sized to accommodate the harvest from a specific vineyard block.

Bottom Left: The Staglin family—Brandon, Shari, Shannon and Garen—work hard to make the best wine they can to support their charitable causes.
Photograph by John McJunkin

Facing Page: Home, sweet home.

The Staglins' donation to the 2006 Napa Valley Auction set an all-time record of $1.05 million, generating more support for the auction's local health care, youth services and low-income housing efforts than any other single lot in the history of worldwide charity wine auctions. "Our goal was to create the ultimate experience for bidders of great generosity," says Garen. " 'Great Wines for Great Causes'—that is what we are all about."

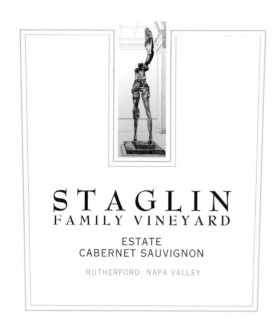

STAGLIN
FAMILY VINEYARD

ESTATE
CABERNET SAUVIGNON

RUTHERFORD, NAPA VALLEY

Stony Hill Vineyard

St. Helena

The first steps on Fred and Eleanor McCrea's trek to the Wine Country were taken in the 1940s when seeking a "country place," not too far from their home in San Francisco. They chose a 160-acre farm once the domain of surefooted goats—a rustic and rocky place of steep angles, perched on the northeast slope of Spring Mountain. Above the fog line, their retreat was the quintessential mountain vineyard location, offering dramatic vistas, rocky soil and cool temperatures resulting in vineyards producing small yields of fruit with magnificent concentrated flavor.

Influenced by several founders of Napa Valley's fledgling wine industry, and having developed a taste for the white wine of Burgundy, the McCreas and their son, Peter, a child at the time, planted six acres of Chardonnay. A few years later, they expanded their petit vineyard, adding several more acres of Chardonnay as well as Pinot Blanc, Semillon, Gewurztraminer and White Riesling. Today, Stony Hill's 42 acres of vineyards wind over the mountain terrain. Vines, in spring's bright leaves, flow like a vivid green river—contrasting with the darker, wild vegetation, thriving beside it.

Only the second winery built in Napa Valley after the end of Prohibition in 1933, Stony Hill produced its first commercial wine in 1952. The grapevine carvings surrounding the cellar door are a quiet tribute to the art within. Stony Hill wines received accolades from the start. Noted French-born wine writer André Simon reportedly compared the Stony Hill Chardonnay to a grand cru of Burgundy.

Top Left: Stony Hill's reputation is built on the elegant, fruity style of its white wines including Chardonnay and Gewurztraminer pictured here. They also make White Riesling and a sweet Semillon.

Bottom Left: The entry to Stony Hill's 55-year-old wine cellar is flanked by grape vine panels carved by founder Fred McCrea.

Facing Page: the terraced White Riesling vineyard was designed in 1947 by the Soil Conservation Service to prevent soil erosion.

Alive with vineyards, flowers and people who are part of Stony Hill, this unassuming estate has aged well, as have the wines produced here. Now, Peter McCrea and his wife, Willinda, run the business, preserving it, in turn, for their children. "This winery is operated one generation at a time," explains Peter, "that is the way we keep it small and personal—operating at a very human level."

Dry-farmed, the vineyard produces only 1.5 tons of fruit per acre. Grapes are harvested into lug baskets and carried to the press for a gentle squeeze rather than a macerating crush. It is difficult to imagine that in 1948, only 200 acres of Chardonnay were planted in the state of California, and six acres of it was at Stony Hill. Fifty years later, over 95,000 acres are planted to Chardonnay in the state.

Winemaker at Stony Hill since 1973, Mike Chelini proudly follows the winemaking style established by Fred McCrea more than 50 years ago. "We aim to achieve balance between the intense fruit of our hillside vineyard and the notable acid that gives the wine structure and aging ability." To avoid "over-produced wines," he buys only a few new barrels each year: "The workhorse barrels are the old 130 gallon barrels I use for fermentation. I don't put the wine through malolactic and I don't stir lees."

Above Left: Proprietors Willinda and Peter McCrea and Brittany Katie Scarlett inspect young Chardonnay vines to see if bloom has begun.

Above Right: Stony Hill's hillside vineyards are surrounded by native forests of maple, dogwood, madrone, Douglas fir, coast redwood, and various species of live and deciduous oak trees.

Facing Page: Stony Hill's historic small winery is framed by Modesto ash trees at the swimming pool.

Stony Hill Vineyard is known for its elegant Chardonnay wines exhibiting notes of apple and citrus along with a mineral quality balanced by a faint hint of oak. For more than 50 years, the McCreas have sold their limited production directly to consumers through a simple newsletter. "We enjoy long-lasting relationships with our customers," says Peter.

Terra Valentine

St. Helena

Peeking through the trees and hillocks on Spring Mountain is a winery castle. The artisan-constructed fieldstone winery is Terra Valentine, presiding over the vineyards of owners Angus and Margaret Wurtele.

Having visited and enjoyed the Napa Valley often over the years, the Wurteles dreamed of owning a vineyard and small winery. In 1995, after a successful career in the paint business in Minnesota, Angus and his wife, Margaret, an accomplished writer and publisher, bought a 75-acre property with a hillside vineyard planted to Cabernet Sauvignon. The 35-acre Wurtele Vineyard is where Angus and Margaret chose to build their home, aptly named Casa Cabernet. As they learned the secrets of grape growing, the couple continued their search for a winery site that appealed to them.

Built in the 1960s, the winery that is now Terra Valentine was designed and constructed by a reclusive, eccentric inventor. A loner, wine sales were difficult, and he was more at home building his architectural masterpiece—doing the stonework and stained glass himself. The many stained glass windows that portray winemaking scenes from Roman and Greek mythology reflect jewel-toned sunlight across the floors and interiors. Matching spiral staircases are equipped with grapevine-sculpted railings and images of grape clusters decorating each step. Following the theme, one of the stairways leads into a full oak cask, with a door leading out the other side. The oak paneling in the tasting salon—originally intended for a famous abode—initially graced a London wine merchant's salon. Taken down, piece by piece, it was shipped to California.

Top Left: Terra Valentine co-owners Angus and Margaret Wurtele.

Bottom Left: Each visitor is treated to an intimate tasting of multiple wines paired with local artisan cheeses and dark chocolate.

Facing Page: Villa Valentine is surrounded by Cabernet Sauvignon vines on the Yverdon Vineyard Estate.

The castle winery had been abandoned for many years and the gardens overgrown, but when the Wurteles first saw it, they were enchanted and particularly charmed by the stained glass window picturing Dionysus on the boat. In 1999, The Wurteles purchased the 80-acre property and named their winery Terra Valentine. Terra, the Latin word for "land," acknowledges the importance of hillside soil in defining mountain wines, while Valentine honors Angus's father, Valentine Wurtele. "They wanted to bring this sleeping storybook castle back to life," says Sam Baxter, winemaker and general manager. "It's a romantic place that inspires people. Many marriage proposals occur here."

At an average elevation of 1,800 to 2,000 feet, the Yverdon Vineyard surrounds the castle winery. The first nine acres were planted in 2001; 18 more acres were planted in 2006-2007. The property is also home to Villa Valentine, a picturesque French country stone guesthouse on the knoll to the east of the winery. Charming, with hand-carved ceiling beams, it offers a magnificent view of the vineyard, St. Helena and Howell Mountain across the valley.

Terra Valentine's flagship wine, the Spring Mountain District Cabernet Sauvignon, is a blend of both their estate vineyards. "The Spring Mountain Cabernet showcases characteristics of both vineyards," says Sam. The lower Wurtele Vineyard, located at 1,000 feet, is warmer in the afternoons, but cooler in the mornings due to the valley fog.

Above: The Wurtele Vineyard Estate planted in 1990 consists of 35 acres of Cabernet Sauvignon.

Facing Page: Stained glass depicting St. Genevieve de Paris overlooks the grand table in the tasting salon.

The grapes provide softer tannins and lush, ripe forward fruit to the blend. Fruit from the higher Yverdon Vineyard, above the fog line at Terra Valentine Winery, gives spice, anise, and more structure and depth. "The reward is producing a wine with intensity that is elegant and approachable. That's what mountain fruit can give you when it's reined in properly," says Sam.

Sam has been with the winery since its inception. "My vision is to produce memorable wines from Spring Mountain—to do the best we can to capture the vineyard, the appellation and the passion of the people involved. When people taste the wine and learn a little bit about it, I want all of that to shine through. I want people to fall in love with Spring Mountain and with our Terra Valentine wines."

Top Left: Captivating stained glass depicts Dionysus on the boat in striking color and detail.

Bottom Left: The fieldstone winery at Terra Valentine.

Facing Page: The view from Villa Valentine down Spring Mountain District to St. Helena.

TERRA VALENTINE

Good things are happening at Terra Valentine. As new life has been brought into the old castle and vineyard, romance has spread through the land, grapes and wine.

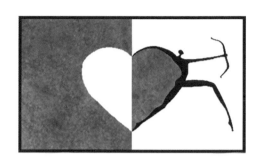

Truchard Vineyards

Napa

The Truchards' entire life changed with the grape—literally. In San Antonio, Texas, when Jo Ann Truchard was pregnant with her fourth child, she slipped on a grape, fell and broke her knee. Four days later, her son was born. Tony Truchard was slated to go to Korea as medical commander; however, due to his wife's condition, he asked for a delay. His orders were subsequently changed to California and their fate became "the grape."

Truchard Vineyards was established in 1974, when the couple came to the Carneros region of the Napa Valley and purchased a 20-acre parcel of land. They transformed what was an abandoned prune orchard into a vineyard and began selling the fruit to a local winery. At the time, Tony was an internist practicing in Reno where the couple lived with their six children. The family drove from Reno on weekends to develop the Napa land into a vineyard.

Tony Truchard's grandfather pioneered the family's winemaking tradition when he came from Lyon, France, in the late 1800s to a small town near Houston, Texas. Here, he bought land and built a state-of-the-art winery building and planted a vineyard; however, the weather was too hot and humid so the grapes became diseased. The winery was converted into a barn. More than 100 years later in Napa Valley, the Truchard's converted their barn into a winery. Their wine label captures this conversion and essence of the vineyards with the blue reservoir that gathers rainwater used for drip irrigation; burnt umber hills rising before a green tree line; volcanic soil blazing red where Syrah and Zinfandel vines flourish; and marine sediment accumulating below the

Top Left: Tony and Jo Ann enjoy a stroll through the mustard.

Middle Left: The gazebo is a perfect place to enjoy a glass of wine.

Bottom Left: The underground cave is the ideal spot to age the red wine in barrels.

Facing Page: Rolling hills of Truchard Vineyards with a portion of the olive trees.

billowing clouds of the Carneros fog; and the barn that brings it all full circle gracing the entire scene.

The Truchard Estate Vineyard has grown to 400 acres, of which 270 are planted. They now sell grapes to more than 20 premiere Napa Valley wineries. Starting in 1989, the Truchards began making wine for themselves using only their estate-grown fruit. Today, they sell 70 percent of their grapes and use 30 percent for their estate wines. The winery was bonded in 1990 and production began at 1,000 cases but quickly outgrew the barn's capacity. Eventually, 11,000 square feet of caves were built into the siltstone to store all the red wine barrels.

With the addition of the wine cave, Truchard now produces 11 different wines totaling 16,000 cases per year. The Truchard signature wine, Chardonnay, is planted throughout the southern part of the Truchard Estate Vineyard, flourishing in the clay soils of the esteemed Carneros grape-growing region.

The Truchard Estate Vineyard is a series of hills and valleys molded by a variety of soils: clay, shale, sandstone, volcanic rock and ash. The various combinations of terrain, geology and marine-moderated temperatures provide unique winegrowing conditions. All the vineyards are sustainably farmed, with a portion being farmed organically.

Above: Many memorable family events occur in the "big room."

Facing Page: Winery, underground caves and Truchard Vineyards.

Truchard wines are produced with the vineyard in mind. "We always will consider ourselves a big vineyard and a small winery," says Truchard. Their handcrafted wines stem from the premium fruit nurtured for more than three decades by Jo Ann and Tony Truchard—forever indebted to "the grape."

Truchard Vineyards

Tudal Family Winery

St. Helena

Tudal Family Winery lies on the northern edge of St. Helena, along the Napa River within the shadow of the eastern mountains. The rustic allure of the property immediately radiates a warm, inviting ambience. Visitors of any age can find something to explore, whether it is the array of Napa Valley wines, the enticing flower and vegetable gardens or the collection of historic farm tractors, tools and bygone novelties that make up a fascinating agricultural retrospective. "It's all real," says owner John Tudal, the son of winery founders Arnold and Alma Tudal. The agricultural artifacts gracing the grounds preserve memories of the Tudals' 75-year background as vegetable farmers in Alameda. A wall of photos in the winery lab where Arnold held court lovingly portrays the many winery visitors and friends (including Joltin' Joe DiMaggio) he charmed over the years.

Founded on 10 acres of land, with advice from Louis P. Martini to plant Cabernet Sauvignon, Tudal Winery was born in 1974. The first vines Arnold planted by hand were in the rocky soil of the ancient riverbed. Now more than 30 years old, these gnarled vines are called the "Old Block." Later, the River Vineyard was planted in the gravelly soil that lies between the winery and the Napa River. In 1978, after years of producing home wine for family and friends, there were enough grapes to make commercial wine on a small scale. "We never intended to go into the wine business," says John, who took over the estate when his parents retired in 2001.

Top Left: Alma Tudal and her son, John, are carrying on the work begun by Arnold Tudal in 1974.

Bottom Left: Tudal is best known for its Bordeaux-style Estate Cabernet Sauvignon and innovative red blends.

Facing Page: Once sold at local produce markets, today the farmed Tudal organic vegetables are served to winery family and guests while the flowers add beauty to the winery house.

Raised on his family's winery property in Oregon, Ron Vuylsteke has been making wine at Tudal for 10 years. Ron learned the Tudal style from Arnold and is carrying on the tradition after his death in 2006. The Tudal Estate Cabernet Sauvignon is made from the home vineyard where grapes grown on three different soil types create a Bordeaux-style wine with notes of violets, blackberries, blueberries and currants.

With the tree-lined Napa River in the background, the eye-catching flower and vegetable gardens are all organically farmed. Lush and overflowing from their raised planters, roses bloom and trumpet vines climb numerous trellises as well as creep over the blue tractor that rests permanently in the flower-filled earth. It is one of the family's old metal plow-horses, saved from rusting in the river. "It was down by the river under the trees," says John. "I got another tractor and pulled it up into the garden."

Parked here and there, are other vintage tractors symbolizing both the family's hard work and the playfulness so evident in the atmosphere at Tudal. The faded red Massey-Harris tractor was bought by John's grandfather, George "Baci" Cerruti, in 1947 and used on the family farms until 1972. "I'm a third generation vegetable farmer," he says. "I was driving tractors on the family farm when I was 10, and then at 16, commercially licensed to drive produce to the San Francisco and Oakland markets." Initially, John parked the tractor as a conversation piece for visitors—at first, to his dad's chagrin. "Then I had an idea," he says, "Tractor. Tractor Red. Tractor Shed Red! I'm going to make Tractor Shed Red! My dad and I laughed together, and now we have a great wine with a distinctive label."

Above: A red Massey-Harris tractor that belonged to John Tudal's grandfather inspired the wine called Tractor Shed Red.

Facing Page: The gray tractor is one of Tudals' old metal plow-horses; now it is a fixture on the grounds.

The tractors and the antique basket press are just a few of the wonderful old-time items that enhance the property, each a center of many stories shared with visitors who are searching for history, connection and down-home friendliness, as well as hand-crafted, limited-production Napa Valley wines sold at reasonable prices. "The legacy of my dad, Arnold Tudal, and the crew

Top Left: The backbone of Tudal Winery: Ron Vuylsteke, Alma, John, Cheryl Stotler and Pablo Ortega.

Bottom Left: Many visitors return to Tudal once they discover the old potting shed serves as the perfect spot for a picnic or barbeque.

Facing Page: In the rocky soil of the ancient riverbed, the Tudals have grown Cabernet grapes for more than 30 years.

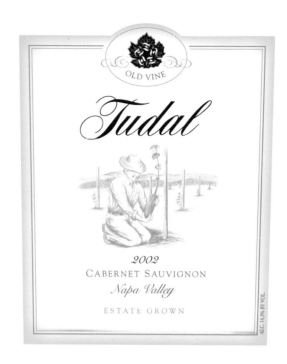

here at the winery, continues to bring people from across the country looking for the essence of what the Napa Valley wine experience used to be," says John. "We have never changed our feel in all these years. Our hearts are here."

ZD Wines

Napa

The founders of ZD wines were shooting for the moon before they landed in Napa Valley. Now, 40 years later, their legacy of world-class wines has been achieved through hard, but much-loved, work that established the roots of three generations deep in the rich soil of Napa Valley. Their love of wine and respect for the land led them to create certified-organic vineyards and to build a winery and visitor center that is warm, welcoming and all about the wine.

ZD Wines was born in the late 1960s, after former aerospace engineers Gino Zepponi and Norman de Leuze helped fulfill America's dream of sending a man to the moon. They named the winery ZD after themselves, but also as a tribute to a reminder posted in all the labs at Aerojet where the two worked, became friends and nurtured their vision: Zero Defects. The aerospace connection is history, but pursuing the legacy of Zero Defects continues to propel three generations of the de Leuze family forward; not toward space, but towards the continuation of a dream that drives them to grow grapes and make wine in a manner that earned them the reputation as one of the major Chardonnay Houses in the Napa Valley.

The organic vineyards surround the ZD Winery. Visitors can stroll the winding herb-lined path leading to the tasting room's tiled courtyard, complete with a splashing fountain and view of the hillsides above. For wine lovers, ending up at the ZD tasting room after a walk through the winery grounds is an anticipated delight. The tasting room is homage not only to the winery's famous Chardonnays, but also to the art of

Top Left: ZDs Wines' organically certified Rutherford Estate Cabernet Sauvignon Vineyard, with mustard in bloom filling the vineyard rows.
Photograph by Lisa Henry

Middle Left: Norman de Leuze, ZD's founding partner, stands in ZD's estate vineyard.
Photograph by © 2004 Bill Tucker

Bottom Left: ZD's private vineyard room is used for exclusive tastings made by appointment: Abacus tastings, cheese and wine seminars and special club member events. The room overlooks the vineyards of Rutherford.

Facing Page: A beautiful meandering path lined with ornamental plantings leads visitors along the ivy-covered winery to the tasting room.

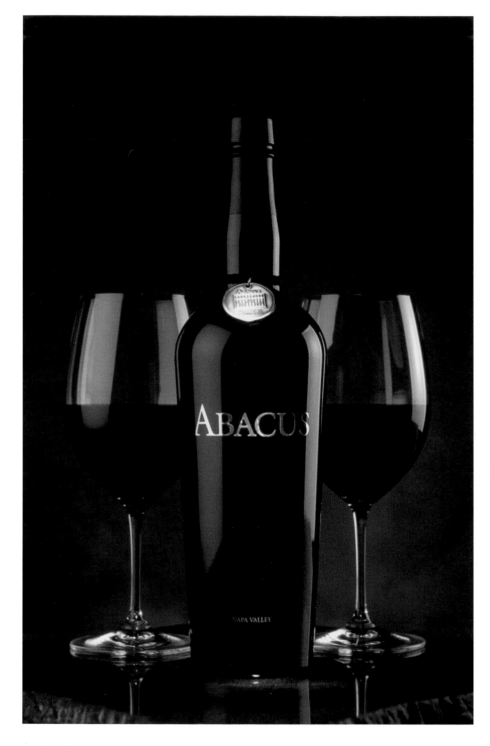

barrel making. The glossy tasting bar, handcrafted from bubinga, an African hardwood, is framed above and below by vertical slats that emulate barrel staves. Across the room the fireplace mirrors the bar's curves and vertical wood design. A unique room, both contemporary and warm, it is a perfect place to relax and enjoy various vintages of ZD wines. For those curious about the well-organized wine library just off the tasting room as well as the winemaking practices and philosophy, winery tours and food and wine pairings are available.

Assistant winemaker Brandon de Leuze is the third generation to contribute his technique to the family tradition. He grew up with the philosophy that great wines start in the vineyard. Brandon, winemaker Chris Pisani and vineyard manager Rafael Llamas are committed to the sustainable and wholesome organic farming practices vital to growing the premium varietals that will be transformed into world-class wines. In effect for many years, these practices are healthy and natural. Rafael blends compost, as well as creates nutritious teas that are applied on the vines. Instead of using herbicides, ZD Wines uses an innovative new machine that, pulled behind a tractor, emits flame close to the ground burning away weeds. This pure method of farming is conscientious stewardship of the earth.

Vintage after vintage, the de Leuze family and winemaker Chris Pisani produce award-winning wines, but one wine, Abacus, is truly without comparison and is every Cabernet Sauvignon-lover's dream. It is a solera-style

Top Left: Abacus, the winery's pinnacle wine. Abacus is described as a solera-style blend of every ZD Reserve Cabernet ever produced.
Photograph by Nanci Kirby

Bottom Left: Three generations of the deLeuze family: (left to right) Robert (CEO and Winemaster), Rosa Lee (Founding Partner), Norman (Founding Partner), Julie (Administrative Director), Brandon (Assistant Winemaker) and Brett (President).
Photograph by Lisa Henry

Facing Page: ZD's tasting room with its rounded architecture reflects the feel of a wine barrel. The room looks into both the winery's extensive library of past vintages and barrel room behind the tasting bar.

red: a wine that combines young and old vintages giving Abacus the maturity of an aged Cabernet with the ripe fruit of youth. Beginning in 1992, ZD started holding back in barrels a small amount of each vintage of their Reserve Cabernet Sauvignon. Each year, 15 percent of the Abacus blend is bottled and released for sale, while 85 percent is returned to the barrel, and the most recent vintage added to the blend. It is unique and ever evolving. The de Leuze family named the wine Abacus after the ancient counting device. Attached to the neck of each bottle is a medallion with an embossed abacus to identify the first and last vintage in the bottle.

At ZD, the Zero Defects philosophy is alive and well.

Publishing Team

Brian G. Carabet, Publisher
John A. Shand, Publisher
Phil Reavis, Executive Publisher
Kathryn Newell, Senior Publisher

Beth Benton, Director of Design & Development
Julia Hoover, Director of Book Marketing & Distribution
Beth Gionta, Editorial Development Specialist

Michele Cunningham-Scott, Art Director
Mary Elizabeth Acree, Graphic Designer
Emily Kattan, Graphic Designer
Ben Quintanilla, Graphic Designer

Rosalie Wilson, Managing Editor
Katrina Autem, Editor
Lauren Castelli, Editor
Anita Kasmar, Editor
Ryan Parr, Editor

Kristy Randall, Managing Production Coordinator
Laura Greenwood, Production Coordinator
Jennifer Lenhart, Production Coordinator
Jessica Garrison, Traffic Coordinator

Carol Kendall, Administrative Manager
Beverly Smith, Administrative Assistant
Carissa Jackson, Sales Support Coordinator
Amanda Mathers, Sales Support Assistant

PANACHE PARTNERS, LLC
CORPORATE OFFICE
13747 Montfort Drive, Suite 100
Dallas, TX 75240
972.661.9884
www.panache.com

NAPA VALLEY OFFICE
856.316.6069

Tudal Family Winery, *page 234*

Chateau Montelena Winery, *page 68*